Barcelona Trav

2023

A Comprehensive Guide to the City's Vibrant

Lifestyle

Luz F. Smith

Table of Content

Introduction to Barcelona

Overview of Barcelona

On the northeastern coast of the Iberian Peninsula in Catalonia, Spain, Barcelona, sometimes known as the "City of Counts," is a bustling and international metropolis. Barcelona, a city with a more than 2,000-year history, effortlessly combines its historic roots with modern innovation, making it one of the most vibrant and culturally varied cities in Europe.

Geographically, Barcelona is tucked between the Collserola mountain range and the Mediterranean Sea, offering locals and guests breathtaking views of the surrounding countryside and a comfortable Mediterranean climate with mild winters and warm summers. The city has a population of over 1.6 million people and covers an area of about 101 square kilometers.

Barcelona's history began in antiquity when it was established as a Roman colony in the first century BC. The city has seen many different civilizations come and go over its history, including the Visigoths, Moors, and Franks. The architecture, culture, and customs of the city have been irrevocably impacted by these factors.

The Sagrada Familia, an incredible basilica created by the great architect Antoni Gaud, is one of Barcelona's most recognizable buildings. The basilica is still being built, with a target completion date of the first half of the twenty-first century. Construction started in 1882. Gaud's distinctive modernist design, marked by minute details, organic curves, and a seamless blending with the natural world, is on display in the Sagrada Familia.

Park Güell, another masterpiece of Gaud's architecture, is located in Barcelona. Public park with plants and architectural features that is a part of the UNESCO World Heritage Site. It is renowned for its vibrant ceramic tiles, distinctive architecture, and whimsical motifs and provides panoramic views of the city.

With several museums, galleries, and theaters dispersed all across the city, Barcelona has a thriving and diverse cultural environment. One of the largest collections of works by the famous Spanish painter Pablo Picasso can be found in the Picasso Museum. Another well-known Catalan artist, Joan Miró, has his paintings on display at the Joan Miró Foundation, showing his avant-garde and surrealist works.

La Rambla, one of Barcelona's most well-known roads, runs from Plaça de Catalunya to the Christopher Columbus Monument in Port Vell and is a busy pedestrian route. La Rambla, a popular destination for both locals and tourists, is lined with cafes, stores, and street entertainers and creates a lively environment. The Barcelona Cathedral is one of the many medieval and Gothic structures that line the maze of narrow streets and squares that make up the nearby Gothic Quarter (Barri Gtic).

The attractive Barceloneta neighborhood, which was formerly a fishing community, is where you can see the city's maritime heritage. With its golden sand beaches, and a variety of seafood restaurants serving delectable paella, and fresh fish, Barceloneta is now a well-liked vacation spot for sunbathers and water sports aficionados.

Barcelona is renowned for its gastronomic scene, which combines traditional Catalan cuisine with cuisines from around the world. The city is home to a large number of Michelin-starred restaurants as well as bustling food markets like the Boqueria Market, where visitors may indulge in a feast of fresh vegetables, seafood, and regional specialties.

Due to the presence of FC Barcelona and RCD Espanyol, two prestigious football clubs, sports are very important in Barcelona. FC Barcelona's home field, the Camp Nou stadium, is one of the biggest football venues in the world and draws ardent supporters from all over the world.

Barcelona has easy access to natural treasures and outdoor activities in addition to its urban allure. Beautiful parks, gardens, and a breathtaking panorama of the city are available at the neighboring Montjuc Hill. About an hour's drive from Barcelona, the mountain range of Montserrat is a well-liked spot for hiking, rock climbing, and sightseeing, including a trip to the abbey where the well-known Black Madonna statue is kept.

Brief History

The vibrant and multicultural city of Barcelona, which is located on Spain's northeastern coast, has a fascinating history that dates back more than two thousand years. Barcelona has seen several changes and left a lasting impression on European history, from its humble beginnings as a Roman town to its emergence as a thriving cultural and economic hub. Take a trip through time as we investigate Barcelona's interesting past.

Barcelona's history may be traced back to antiquity when it was known as Barcino. Due to its advantageous natural harbor and strategic location, Barcino, which was established by the Romans in the first century BC, quickly gained significance. The expansion of the city was facilitated by the Roman construction of fortifications, temples, and other buildings.

Following the collapse of the Western Roman Empire, Barcelona experienced a period of decline and vulnerability as it came under the rule of numerous invading groups, notably the Visigoths and the Moors. The Carolingian monarchy brought about a renaissance in Barcelona in the ninth century, nevertheless. Barcelona's declaration of independence and establishment as the County of Barcelona's capital were both greatly aided by Count Wilfred the Hairy.

Barcelona prospered as a key Mediterranean commerce hub and the epicenter of Catalan culture during the Middle Ages. Particularly during the time of the Catalan-Aragonese confederation, the city's naval prowess allowed it to conduct substantial trade with other Mediterranean nations. Significant political and economic advantages resulted from the union of Barcelona and Aragon in the 12th century, which helped Barcelona reach new levels of wealth.

Christopher Columbus' arrival in Barcelona at the end of the 15th century was one of the pivotal moments in the city's history. By acting as the starting point for several of Columbus's expeditions, Barcelona came to represent the exploration and settlement of the New World. Buildings like the Gothic Quarter and the Columbus Monument were built as a result of the income this business produced, which supported Barcelona's expansion.

For Barcelona, the 19th century was a time of considerable development and upheaval. Rapid urbanization and the creation of an industrial proletariat were two effects of the Industrial Revolution that raced across the metropolis. As the workers' movements grew and the fight for Catalan autonomy intensified, Barcelona emerged as a hub of political and social agitation. Barcelona's cultural importance was further increased by the influence of well-known people like Antoni Gaud, whose architectural wonders dot the cityscape.

Political upheaval and the Spanish Civil War made the 20th century turbulent for Barcelona. The city suffered under General Francisco Franco's oppressive rule, which aimed to stifle Catalan identity and cultural expression. But after Franco died in 1975 and the subsequent shift to democracy, Barcelona had a stunning revival.

Barcelona's development into a contemporary, vibrant city was demonstrated by its hosting of the 1992 Summer Olympics. With the creation of new infrastructure, parks, and the recognizable Olympic Village, the Olympic Games sparked considerable urban renovation. Barcelona established the foundation for its development into a major cultural and tourist destination by becoming a global icon of architectural innovation and urban planning.

Barcelona has remained a thriving hub for innovation, art, and creativity in recent decades. Iconic landmarks like the Sagrada Familia and the Montjuc Communications Tower are prominent features of the city's modern skyline. The city's thriving street culture, world-class dining options, and fervent football tradition all add to its attraction.

Barcelona serves as a symbol of the perseverance of a city that has accepted change and triumphed over adversity today. Barcelona is a mesmerizing location that draws tourists from all over the world because of its rich history, which blends Roman roots, medieval beauty, and modern accomplishments.

Getting To Barcelona

Getting to Barcelona is a thrilling journey that can be completed through a variety of modes of transportation. Barcelona offers a variety of transportation options to fit your interests and needs, whether you choose to fly, drive, take the train, or even combine various modes of transportation. We will examine each method of transportation in detail in the guide that follows and provide you with the knowledge you need to efficiently plan your trip.

Fly to Barcelona

Barcelona is served by Barcelona-El Prat Airport (BCN), a significant hub for both local and international travel. From numerous cities across the world, many airlines provide direct flights to Barcelona. Trains, buses, and taxis are all excellent options for getting from the airport to the city center. By train or bus, it takes roughly 30 minutes to travel from the airport to the city center.

Reaching Barcelona by car

Driving to Barcelona can be a wonderful alternative if you enjoy road trips or have the freedom to stop at different places along the way. Due to its connection to the European road system, Barcelona is reachable from nearby nations. Barcelona is connected to France and other Spanish cities via major roads including the AP-7 and A-2. It's critical to plan your route appropriately because the length of the trip and the route rely on your starting point. Barcelona offers a variety of parking alternatives, including on-street parking and parking in public garages, but be mindful of parking rules and prices.

Train ride to Barcelona

Train travel from Barcelona to major European destinations is convenient, picturesque, and comfortable. Spain's national rail corporation, Renfe, runs AVE high-speed trains that link Barcelona to other Spanish cities including Madrid and Valencia. By using the AVE, you may travel from Madrid to Barcelona in around 2.5 hours. Barcelona has access to both domestic and international rail networks, including the Eurostar, which connects it to places like Paris and Zurich.

Boarding a bus to get to Barcelona

Bus travel is a cheap way to get to Barcelona, especially for those traveling small distances or on a budget. Long-distance bus services from several

European locations to Barcelona are offered by several operators. It is simple to visit the city's attractions upon arrival thanks to the central location of Barcelona's bus terminals. Though depending on the distance, bus journey times can differ from those of other forms of transportation.

Modal combination

Using many means of transportation to go to Barcelona is an additional choice. You could fly to Barcelona and then rent a car to tour the area, or you could take the train to get to nearby cities. With this strategy, you may take advantage of air travel's convenience while still having access to ground transportation's flexibility.

Chapter 1

Planning Your Trip

Best Time to Visit

Barcelona, the energetic capital of Catalonia in Spain, is a city that provides an incredible fusion of history, culture, and stunning architecture. Every traveler may find something to enjoy in Barcelona, whether they are drawn to the city by its breathtaking beaches, first-rate cuisine, or famous sites. But when is the ideal time to travel to this alluring city? To aid in your decision-making, let's examine the various seasons and occasions.

Spring (March to May)

Barcelona's awakening from its winter slumber in the spring is a magical time of year. Temperatures start to rise, averaging between 15 and 20 degrees

Celsius (59 and 68 degrees Fahrenheit). The parks and gardens bloom with vivid colors, and the streets are alive with a sense of rebirth, bringing the city to life. Barcelona's outdoor attractions, such as Park Güell and Montjuc, are perfect to explore in the spring before the summer season's throngs arrive. On April 23, you may also see the traditional Catalan celebration of Sant Jordi, during which the streets are decorated with flowers and books to create a special mood.

The summer (June through August)
Barcelona's busiest travel period is unquestionably the summer and for good reason. Temperatures in the city typically range from 77 to 86 degrees Fahrenheit and are warmed by the Mediterranean sun between 25 and 30 degrees Celsius. Locals and visitors alike follow the call of the beaches to the Mediterranean Sea's coasts to enjoy the warm weather and cool waves. The exuberant Gràcia Festival, which takes place in August and transforms the Gràcia neighborhood's streets into a

riot of color, live music, and street performances, is just one of the many festivals and events that the summer season has to offer. Remember that summer is the biggest season, so plan for more crowds and more expensive tickets.

The autumn season (September through November)

The change from the sweltering heat of summer to colder temps in Barcelona throughout the fall is welcome. Temperatures range from 15 to 25 degrees Celsius (59 to 77 degrees Fahrenheit), which is still considered to be pleasant. This time of year is ideal for discovering the city's architectural marvels, such as the breathtaking Sagrada Familia and the Gothic Quarter, without having to brave the sweltering summer heat or the busiest tourist season. Autumn also ushers in several cultural occasions, such as the Barcelona International Jazz Festival in October and the Barcelona Manga Fair in November, which draw visitors from all over the world who are fans of both music and animation.

Winter (December to February)

Although Barcelona's winters are relatively warm compared to other European cities, with average temperatures between 8 and 15 degrees Celsius (46 and 59 degrees Fahrenheit), it is the slowest time of year for tourists. Winter can be your best option if you want a more relaxing experience. With fewer visitors and shorter wait times at major attractions, the city has a pleasant atmosphere. Top-notch museums like the Picasso Museum and the National Art Museum of Catalonia (MNAC) can be explored at your speed. In addition, Barcelona's Christmas celebrations and markets, particularly the Fira de Santa Llucia, lend the city a festive air.

Duration of Stay

Planning the length of your stay in Barcelona necessitates carefully taking into account several variables, including your interests, free time, and financial situation. Barcelona has plenty to offer everyone, regardless matter whether you're here for a few days or a few months. To assist you in choosing the optimal length of stay in Barcelona, we will examine several choices and offer advice.

A minimum stay of three to four days is advised to experience Barcelona to the fullest. During this time, you can see the city's well-known attractions, eat its delectable cuisine, and take in its distinctive ambiance. Nevertheless, if you have more time on your hands, extending your stay to a week or even longer will give you the chance to explore the city's attractions in greater detail and provide you the freedom to travel outside of its bounds.

Day 1: Spend your first day exploring the city after arriving. Visit the Gothic Quarter, which features lovely squares, winding ancient lanes, and the magnificent Barcelona Cathedral. Discover the colorful La Rambla, a lively pedestrian area populated with stores, eateries, and street performers. Enjoy a leisurely dinner in the evening at a traditional Catalan restaurant.

Day 2: Explore Barcelona's architectural marvels. Visit the Sagrada Familia, an architectural wonder by Antoni Gaud, first thing in the morning. Admire the historic basilica's exquisite craftsmanship and breathtaking design. After that, visit Park Güell, another masterpiece by Gaud, which is renowned for its mosaic tiles made of vibrant colors and panoramic views of the city. Enjoy some delectable seafood while taking a stroll along the beachside promenade in the evening.

Day 3: Discover Barcelona's artistic side. Visit the Pablo Picasso Museum, which is devoted to the creations of the great artist. Explore the trendy El Born district, which is popular for its shops and art galleries. Visit Montjuc Hill in the afternoon to see the Montjuc Olympic Stadium, the Magic Fountain, and the Montjuc Castle. Visit the lively La Boqueria food market to cap off your day with a taste of some of the regional specialties.

Day 4: Travel outside the city and spend the day in the adjacent Montserrat Mountain. Take a picturesque train ride to this breathtaking natural wonder, which is renowned for its serrated rock formations, and the Montserrat Abbey, which is where the famed Black Madonna resides. Enjoy scenic hikes, hiking trails, and a quiet retreat from the bustle of the city.

Day 5: Exploring Barcelona's thriving districts. Known for its bohemian vibe, quaint squares, and exciting nightlife, the trendy Gràcia neighborhood is a great place to spend the day. Relax in the lush surroundings of Barcelona's largest park, Park de la Ciutadella. Shop to your heart's content on the fashionable Passeig de Gràcia, which is lined with expensive boutiques and recognizable architectural features.

Day 6: Learn about the maritime history of the city. Explore the Maritime Museum and take a stroll along the waterfront when you visit the historic Port Vell. Discover the vibrant beach bars, sand-filled eateries, and neighborhood of Barceloneta. To see Barcelona's shoreline from a different angle, think about renting a kayak or going on a boat excursion.

Day 7: Those with extra time might want to consider going outside of Barcelona. Take a day trip to the Penedès wine area, where you can tour vineyards, taste regional wines, and take in the stunning scenery. Visit Sitges instead; it's a picturesque coastal town well known for its stunning beaches, thriving art scene, and LGBTQ+ community.

Beyond a week: If you have more time than a week, Barcelona is a great place to base yourself for further exploration because it is so close to other European cities. Take a high-speed rail to the Spanish capital of Madrid or a quick trip to one of the attractive cities in southern France, like Nice or Marseille.

Entry Requirements and Visa Information

Understanding the entry procedures and visa information is crucial when making travel arrangements to Barcelona to guarantee a hassle-free vacation. This tutorial will provide you with an overview of the required paperwork and processes that you need to be familiar with.

Conditions for Entry

1. Validity of passport: You must have a passport that is currently valid to enter Barcelona. Make sure your passport is still valid for at least six months after the day you intend to depart.

2. Visa Exemptions: Visas are not required for citizens of a select group of nations for transitory trips to Spain, including Barcelona. The majority of the European Union's member states, as well as the United States, Canada, Australia, and the United Kingdom, are among these nations. Depending on your nationality, different lengths of stay are permitted under the visa exemption.

3. Schengen Area: Barcelona is a member of the Schengen Area, a group of 26 nations in Europe without internal border controls. You require a Schengen visa if you intend to go to Barcelona and other Schengen nations.

Details about the visa

You must obtain a Schengen visa in advance of traveling to Barcelona if you are a citizen of a nation that needs one. You are permitted to travel to and remain in Barcelona for up to 90 days within 180 days with a Schengen visa. Typically, the following phases are included in the application process:

a. Application: Complete the Schengen visa application honestly and completely. The Spanish embassy or consulate in your nation can provide you with the form, as can their internet resource.

b. Required Documents: In addition to the application form, you must submit proof of your intended purpose for visiting (such as an invitation letter, hotel reservations, or registration for a conference), a valid passport, passport-sized photos, a travel itinerary, proof of lodging, proof of travel insurance, and proof of your financial ability.

c. Visa Fee: Pay the required visa fee, which varies based on your country of citizenship and the type of visa you are requesting. Even if your application is denied, keep in mind that the cost is not refundable.

d. Appointment: Make an appointment at the Spanish embassy or consulate in your native country to present your application and biometric information (fingerprints and a photo).

e. Processing Time: The time needed to complete a Schengen visa varies, but it typically takes about 15 days. Applying long before the dates of your anticipated travel is advised.

f. Interview: In some circumstances, an interview at the embassy or consulate may be needed of you. Usually, this is done to provide further evidence or to clarify something.

1. Long-Term Visas: If you intend to stay in Barcelona for some time longer than 90 days or if you have a particular reason for doing so, such as employment, study, or family reunion, you must apply for a long-term visa or a residence permit. Depending on your circumstances, the long-term visa requirements and application procedure may change. It is advised to get in touch with the

Spanish embassy or consulate in your country of residence for more information and support.

2. Citizens of the EU/EEA: Without a visa, you are permitted to live, work, and study in Barcelona if you are a citizen of one of the member countries of the Switzerland, the European Economic Area, or the European Union (EU).However, to receive a residency certificate, you might need to register with the local government after you arrive.

The process for obtaining a visa can alter over time, thus it is advised to check the official website of the Spanish embassy or consulate in your country for the most recent and correct information. Additionally, give yourself enough time to gather all the required paperwork and finish the application procedure to avoid any last-minute issues.

You may assure a smooth and comfortable visit to this fascinating city by being aware of Barcelona's admission regulations and visa information. Prepare in advance, obtain the necessary paperwork, and confidently start your vacation in Barcelona.

Travel Insurance

Knowing how to use travel insurance

A type of coverage known as travel insurance offers financial security against unforeseen circumstances that could arise before or during your journey. It often provides support in the event of a travel cancellation or interruption, a medical emergency lost or delayed luggage, and other unanticipated events. With travel insurance, you can rest easy knowing that should an unforeseen situation interfere with your plans, you will be financially protected.

Details of Coverage

a) vacation Cancellation or Interruption: This coverage pays out non-refundable costs if your vacation is cut short or canceled for particular reasons including illness, injury, or unforeseeable occurrences like terrorist attacks or natural disasters.

b) Medical Costs: Travel insurance covers medical emergencies, which is important while visiting a foreign country. Usually, it pays for things like hospital bills, prescriptions, and emergency medical transportation.

c) Baggage and Personal Belongings: This coverage guard against the loss, robbery, or destruction of your luggage and other personal effects. It offers you financial support for any necessary products you might use on your journey.

d) Travel Delay: If your vacation is postponed due to events beyond your control (such as bad weather or airline strikes), travel insurance may be able to help cover additional costs for lodging, food, and transportation.

e) Personal Liability: This insurance covers you if, while traveling, you unintentionally harm someone or damage their property. It might assist with settlements or litigation costs.

Selecting the Best Policy

Take these things into account while choosing travel insurance for your trip to Barcelona:

a) Coverage Limits: Verify that the policy provides sufficient coverage for medical costs, travel cancellations, lost baggage, and other potential risks.

b) Pre-existing medical conditions: If you have any, find out if the insurance policy covers them or if you need additional coverage.

c) Trip Duration: Check to see if the policy covers the full length of your trip, especially if you want to stay longer or partake in activities that are not typically covered by plans.

d) Activities and Sports: Check your policy to see if it covers the activities you intend to engage in and if you intend to engage in adventurous activities or sports.

Comparing Insurance Companies

Compare multiple insurance companies using the following standards to determine which one offers the best travel insurance for your Barcelona trip:

a) Reputation and client Reviews: To confirm an insurance company's dependability and client contentment, investigate and assess its reputation and customer reviews.

b) Coverage Options: Research several insurance companies' coverage options, policy limitations, and exclusions to choose which one best suits your requirements.

c) *Cost and Value:* Take into account the premium cost and the value provided by the insurance policy in terms of benefits and coverage.

d) *Customer Support:* Consider the caliber and accessibility of the customer support services offered by insurance providers, especially emergency assistance.

Chapter 2

Essential Travel Information

Currency and Money Matters

Since the Romans founded Barcelona in the first century BC, it has long been a center of trade and business. The sestertius was a little bronze coin used as money during the Roman era. The coinage changed to the tremissis, a gold coin, in the fifth century as the Roman Empire crumbled and Barcelona came under Visigothic authority. However, Islamic dinars and dirhams were adopted during the Arab invasion of the area in the eighth century, indicating the influence of Muslim civilization.

With the rise of the Catalan-Aragonese Crown in the 12th century, Barcelona's economic history underwent a sea change. Barcelona benefited greatly from the affluence that the Crown, which included Catalonia, Aragon, Valencia, and the Balearic Islands, brought. The Barcelona pound, also known as the pleura, a silver coin that was widely used in Mediterranean trade, served as the currency of the Crown.

Barcelona saw the Renaixença, or Golden Age, in the 14th and 15th centuries. A flourishing of the arts, culture, and trade during this period increased Barcelona's financial activity. A variety of currencies, notably the lliura, the gold florin from Florence, and the Venetian ducat supported trade and commerce internationally and powered the economy.

As Barcelona developed into a significant port for colonial trade in the 16th century as a result of Spain's conquest of the Americas, it amassed enormous wealth. The New World's influx of silver and gold prompted the creation of the Casa de la

Contratación, a trading agency in charge of policing trade with the colonies. The Spanish real, a silver coin manufactured in Barcelona and other Spanish cities, served as the country's unit of exchange at the time.

Money and currency in Barcelona underwent substantial alterations in the 19th century. The Spanish real was replaced as the country's official currency with the peseta in 1868. Barcelona adopted the peseta, which served as the country's currency until the euro was introduced in 2002.

Barcelona experienced a turbulent 20th century that was characterized by political unrest, economic hardships, and the Spanish Civil War. Barcelona was able to repair and revive its economy in the second half of the century despite these obstacles. As a result of the rise of industries including manufacturing, textiles, tourism, and services, the city developed into a significant industrial and commercial hub.

Barcelona established a strong banking industry to support its economic activity in terms of money matters. Banco de Barcelona and Banco Sabadell, two significant Spanish banks, established presences in the city. These financial organizations offered a variety of services, like loans, mortgages, and investment opportunities, which helped Barcelona's economy grow and expand.

Barcelona further assimilated into the world economy with the creation of the European Union. The 1992 Olympic Games in the city acted as a stimulus for infrastructure growth, urban renovation, and global prominence. The economy of Barcelona grew rapidly, bringing in foreign capital and making it a popular tourist destination.

The 2002 introduction of the euro simplified monetary issues in Barcelona. Spain adopted the euro as its official currency, replacing the peseta as a unit of exchange. This change promoted economic unity and stability by facilitating trade, travel, and financial activities throughout the Eurozone.

Today, the tourism industry, services, technology, and innovation are major contributors to Barcelona's economy. Millions of tourists come to the city year, bringing in money and creating jobs. Barcelona's economy continues to be significantly supported by the financial industry, which offers a wide range of financial services to both consumers and corporations through regional and international institutions.

The future of Barcelona's currency and financial affairs is entwined with the state of the world economy, to look ahead. Barcelona will continue to use the euro as its official currency as a part of the Eurozone, taking advantage of its advantages and stability. The financial dynamics of the city may be impacted by prospective problems like economic swings, technology disruptions, and geopolitical changes, necessitating adaptation, and resilience.

Language and Communication

Catalan is the official language of Barcelona as well as the larger region of Catalonia. Although it is a Romance language like Spanish, French, and Italian, Catalan also has its unique features. Schools, governmental organizations, and the media all use it as their major language of instruction. Catalans have a strong sense of pride in their language and see it as an essential component of their cultural identity. Catalan predominates in daily life, as seen by the fact that signs, official papers, and public announcements are frequently written in it.

But it's crucial to remember that Barcelona is a global city that welcomes millions of tourists every year from all over the world. As a result, Barcelona has a large Spanish-speaking population that speaks and understands Castilian. Many residents are multilingual in Catalan and Spanish, and it is typical to move between the two depending on the situation or the preferences of the interlocutors. In commercial settings, dining establishments, and contacts with tourists, Spanish is frequently spoken.

English is a language that is frequently spoken in Barcelona together with Catalan and Spanish, especially among younger people and in tourist districts. English proficiency is becoming more and more in demand due to the city's multicultural makeup, popularity as a tourist destination, and importance as a commercial and business center. Many residents, especially those employed in the tourism sector, speak English well and can interact with tourists.

Barcelona is home to many immigrant populations, each with its unique linguistic traditions, in addition to the three main languages spoken there. Barcelona is now home to communities from Latin America, North Africa, Sub-Saharan Africa, and other regions of Europe. These communities brought a wide variety of languages with them, including Arabic, French, Italian, Portuguese, Chinese, and more. Although these languages are not as common as Catalan, Spanish, or English, they still add to the linguistic diversity of the city and enhance its multicultural atmosphere.

Beyond spoken languages, Barcelona is linguistically diverse. The area is well-known for its thriving street art community, where artistic ideas and messages are frequently expressed through visual mediums. The local community's cultural and socioeconomic ideas are reflected through street installations like graffiti, murals, and street art. Even though Catalan and Spanish are regularly employed, these art forms transcend linguistic barriers by frequently combining universal symbols and images to convey their themes.

The literary scene in Barcelona is also thriving. Catalonia has produced important works in both Catalan and Spanish thanks to the many well-known authors and poets that have come from there. Readers, writers, and literary aficionados from all over the world come to the city to attend literary festivals, book fairs, and cultural events that honor the written word. Barcelona has a rich literary history and a diverse population, which together contribute to a thriving literary environment where several languages coexist and inspire one another.

Barcelona and other Spanish-speaking countries have many things in common when it comes to communication etiquette. Handshakes and cheek kisses are standard means of welcome among acquaintances. Greetings are often warm and cordial. Unless otherwise requested, formal addresses should be made to people using their titles or last names. Politeness and respect are highly prized, and making an effort to speak some basic Catalan words can go a long way in fostering good relationships with the locals.

Safety Tips

Like visiting any other large city, it's crucial to be aware of safety precautions to make your trip enjoyable and secure. Here are some crucial safety recommendations to remember while visiting or living in Barcelona.

1. Be careful with your possessions: Pickpockets and petty criminals sometimes target travelers in Barcelona, as in many other well-known tourist locations. Wallets, phones, and other valuables should be kept in a bag that may be carried across the body or in a front pocket. Keep valuable jewels and big quantities of cash hidden.

2. Be vigilant in crowded areas: Pickpockets may target busy markets, well-traveled tourist destinations, and transportation hubs. Be mindful of your surroundings and exercise caution, especially in crowded situations. Try not to be distracted by people approaching you or live entertainment on the street.

3. Take a dependable mode of transportation: Barcelona's bus and metro systems are both effective modes of public transit. utilize trustworthy ride-hailing services or only utilize licensed taxis. If you decide to rent a vehicle, make sure to leave any valuables outside and park them in well-lit places.

4. Watch out for scams: Be wary of those who offer assistance without asking for it, especially near tourist attractions. Distracting tactics, phony petitions, and unlicensed tour guides are examples of common scams. Refuse politely and go about your business.

5. Stay in well-lit and populous locations: Barcelona is typically safe, but it's best to avoid getting lost at night and stick to well-lit and frequented areas. Avoid going for a solo stroll in darkened or empty regions. If at all possible, go on a trip with someone or in a group.

6. Respect local laws and customs: Get to know local laws and customs to avoid misunderstandings or legal problems. It's vital to observe the rules specific to Barcelona. For instance, it is illegal to drink in public in some places and it is forbidden to smoke in many public areas.

7. official Tourist information: use official tourist information centers or the concierge at your hotel for assistance or information if necessary. They can offer trustworthy advice and suggestions for risk-free areas to explore.

8. Exercise caution when using ATMs: Select machines that are close to populated areas that are well-lit. As you input your PIN, cover the keypad. Also, keep an eye out for any suspicious activity or opportunistic bystanders. Use the ATMs inside banks if at all possible.

9. Protect your lodgings: Take basic safety precautions whether you're staying in a hotel, hostel, or vacation home. Use the hotel's main door as opposed to side entrances or back alleyways, lock your apartment or room when you leave, and keep valuables in a safe or secure location.

10. Emergency Number: Save local emergency contacts and phone numbers, such as those for the police, ambulance, and your embassy or consulate. It's critical to keep these numbers nearby in case of an emergency or if you need help.

11. Keep up with local news and advisories: Before leaving, look up any travel warnings or alerts issued for Barcelona. Keep up with local news to learn about any recent safety concerns or events that may have an impact on your stay.

12. Obey beach safety regulations: The beaches around Barcelona's shoreline are world-famous. However, it's important to abide by beach safety rules, such as swimming only in authorized areas and paying attention to warning signs. Follow lifeguard recommendations, stay wary of strong currents, and keep an eye on your personal property.

Remember that the purpose of these safety recommendations is to improve your trip to Barcelona and guarantee your safety. You may safely and securely take in the city's attractions and make lifelong experiences by being alert, being prepared, and employing common sense.

First aid Equipment and uses

Being ready for any unanticipated medical problems or mishaps is crucial when visiting Barcelona. To protect your safety and the well-being of your fellow passengers, it is advisable to have a first aid bag that is well-stocked. You can travel about Barcelona with confidence after reading this guide's description of some necessary first aid supplies and their functions.

1. Adhesive bandages: These are used to wrap up minor cuts, blisters, or abrasions to prevent infection and promote healing.

2. Sterile gauze pads: These are excellent for cleaning and covering bigger wounds, preventing contamination, and fostering healthy healing.

3. Adhesive tape: This substance holds dressings, bandages, or splints in place, protecting the damaged region and keeping it stable.

4. Disinfecting wipes: These is known as "antiseptics" are essential for cleansing wounds, preventing infection, and upholding proper hygiene.

5. Antiseptic solution: These treatments, such as hydrogen peroxide or povidone-iodine, are efficient for cleaning wounds and halting bacterial development.

6. Tweezers: Tweezers are handy for removing splinters, thorns, or other things that have become embedded in the skin.

7. Scissors: When administering first aid, you can cut tape, gauze, or clothing with a small pair of scissors.

6. Disposable gloves: These are essential for preventing infection in both you and the injured party. For those who have latex allergies, latex-free gloves are advised.

7. Instant cold packs: These are used to alleviate pain and swelling after minor injuries like sprains or strains.

8. Triangular bandages: These functional bandages can be used as big dressings for head wounds or as slings to restrain wounded limbs.

9. A CPR mask with a one-way valve: Creates a barrier between the rescuer and the victim, making it possible to administer cardiopulmonary resuscitation safely.

10. Safety pins: Are useful for constructing impromptu slings and fastening bandages.

11. Thermometer: A digital thermometer enables you to track your body's temperature and spot fever or hypothermia symptoms.

12. Painkillers: Over-the-counter painkillers like acetaminophen or ibuprofen can help with minor aches, pains, or headaches.

13. Antihistamines: These medications can be used to treat allergic reactions or offer comfort in cases of bug bites or stings.

14. Sunscreen: Because Barcelona is known for its sunny weather, it's important to shield your skin from UV radiation. Be sure to always have a broad-spectrum sunscreen on hand.

15. Oral rehydration salts: These salts can help replenish electrolytes and restore enough hydration if you become dehydrated due to illness or severe heat.

16. Medical adhesive tape: This tape is intended for use in attaching bandages and dressings in regions that are prone to moisture or movement.

17. Eyewash solution: In cases of contamination or eye irritation, an eyewash solution can flush out foreign objects and provide symptomatic relief.

18. First aid manual: It's crucial to have a detailed manual that explains the fundamentals of first aid procedures so you can react appropriately in an emergency.

Remember, it's essential to become familiar with these items' uses and acquire a foundational understanding of first aid before your journey. To get useful knowledge and assurance addressing medical crises, think about taking a first aid course. To provide urgent care until professional medical help is available, a well-stocked first aid bag, knowledge, and prompt action can make a big difference.

Travel kits

Clothing

The Mediterranean climate that Barcelona experiences is characterized by moderate winters and hot summers. Bring summer-appropriate attire that is light and breathable. T-shirts, shorts, dresses, skirts, and light pants are necessities. For chilly evenings, especially in the spring and fall, don't forget to carry a lightweight jacket or cardigan. If you intend to make use of Barcelona's stunning beaches, pack a beach towel and swimwear

Footwear

Comfortable footwear is essential in Barcelona because of how much walking there will likely be.Select a pair of sturdy, supportive sneakers or walking shoes.For trips to the beach or hot summer days, sandals or flip-flops are also necessary.

Accessories

It's important to protect oneself from the sun, so bring a hat or cap with a wide brim. Sunglasses and high-SPF sunscreen are essential. Bring dressier attire and some accessories if you plan to go out at night because Barcelona has a thriving nightlife.

Electronics

Make sure you have the gadgets you need for connecting and recording memories. Barcelona's beautiful architecture must be captured with a digital camera or a smartphone with an excellent camera. Remember to pack charging cords, a power adapter (if required), and a portable charger to keep your electronics charged all day.

Documents for travel

Keep in mind to secure all of your travel papers. This includes all of your critical papers, such as your passport, any necessary visas, travel insurance, hotel bookings, and other papers. A physical copy and an electronic backup should both be present in case of loss or theft.

Financial and banking

Bring enough cash or a credit/debit card to cover your spending because Barcelona is a member of the Eurozone. Inform your bank or credit card provider in advance of your vacation intentions to prevent any problems with money access. To protect your belongings, it's also a good idea to travel with a money belt or a lockable wallet.

.

Medicines and general health

Make sure you have enough of any prescription medications you take to last the duration of your vacation. It's a good idea to always have a small first-aid kit with you, complete with bandages, painkillers, antiseptic wipes, and any other personal prescriptions or medical supplies you might require.

Essentials for travel

Pack a few useful items to enhance your touring experience. A city map or guidebook, a pocket-sized umbrella for unforeseen downpours, a small backpack or tote bag for transporting your items during the day, and a reusable water bottle are a few examples.

Communication and Language

Although English is commonly spoken in Barcelona, it never hurts to have a basic understanding of the local tongue. To make it easier to communicate with natives, think about bringing a little phrasebook or using a translation app.

Miscellaneous

Last but not least, think about taking a few extra goods that will make your trip more enjoyable. For lengthy flights, these might include a foldable travel pillow, sleep aids like earplugs and eye masks, and a book or e-reader for downtime reading.

Local Customs and Etiquette

Your experience as a guest can be substantially improved by comprehending and observing these practices. Here are some essential components of Barcelonan culture and manners:

1. Greetings and Personal Space: A handshake is the most typical way to greet someone when you first meet them in Barcelona, while close friends and family members may kiss each other on the cheek. Particularly during first meetings, it's critical to respect personal space and refrain from intruding on it.

2. Punctuality: In Barcelona, being on time is highly regarded. It's preferable to appear on time for appointments, meetings, and social occasions because it's considered rude to keep people waiting.

3.Dress Modestly: Barcelona has a somewhat relaxed dress code. Wearing beachwear or other revealing apparel is not advised when visiting religious locations or more affluent venues. Instead, dress modestly.

4. Dining Etiquette: Dining is a prized social event in Barcelona. It's customary to bring a little gift, like a bottle of wine or some chocolates, to a residence when you're welcome. Furthermore, it is courteous to wait for the host to start eating before beginning your dinner. If the service charge is not included, tipping at restaurants typically ranges between 10 and 15 percent.

5. Language: The native tongue of Catalonia is Catalan, despite Spanish being extensively used in Barcelona. When tourists attempt to say "Bon dia" (Good morning) or "Gràcies" (Thank you) in Catalan, the locals are appreciative.

6. Siesta and Store Hours: Barcelona follows the custom of the siesta, a midday break, like many other Spanish cities. Many stores and companies may close during this time for a few hours. It's critical to arrange your activities appropriately and to observe the local timetable.

7. Festivals and Celebrations: Throughout the year, Barcelona is home to several festivals, including La Mercè and Sant Jordi. These celebrations hold a special place in Catalan culture, and the residents take great delight in them. It's a wonderful chance to get involved in the festivities and learn about the customs of the area.

8. Tipping: Although it is not as widespread in Spain as it is in some other nations, Barcelona does appreciate it. A little gratuity is typically given to tour guides, taxi drivers, and hotel personnel in addition to restaurants as a sign of appreciation for their assistance.

9. Respect for Cultural Divergences: Barcelona is a cosmopolitan and diversified city. You should show respect for the diverse cultures and practices you come across. Be careful not to generalize or stereotype someone based on their ethnicity or nationality.

10. Public Behavior: It's important to be considerate of your actions when in public places. Be careful not to disturb the serenity and quiet of the area with loud conversations, excessive demonstrations of affection, or any other behavior.

11. Public Transportation: Barcelona boasts a robust system of buses and metros for getting about town. It is courteous to give the elderly, expectant mothers, or individuals with impairments your seat when using public transportation. The practice of allowing passengers to exit the car before boarding is also common.

12. Smoking Restrictions: Smoking is not permitted in a lot of indoor public areas, including pubs, restaurants, and lodging facilities. Observe specified smoking places, and show consideration for non-smokers.

You will not only have a more pleasant visit if you observe Barcelona's customs and etiquette, but you will also encourage positive interactions with people and develop a stronger bond with the city and its rich cultural legacy.

Chapter 3

Top Attractions

Sagrada Familia

All who see the Sagrada Familia are captivated by its breathtaking beauty. It stands tall and proud in the center of Barcelona. The famed Antoni Gaud's architectural masterpiece, which has become a must-see destination for travelers from all over the world, is now recognized as the city's symbol. The Sagrada Familia provides an amazing experience that combines art, spirituality, and pure amazement with its ornate façade, lofty towers, and captivating interior.

- Outside splendor

  A breathtaking display of complex stone carvings, ornate spires, and bright stained glass windows welcomes visitors as they approach the Sagrada Familia. Each facade has a unique narrative that is illustrated by biblical scenes and displays Gaud's creative genius. With its ornately decorated sculptures and organic designs, the Nativity Façade both represents and imparts a profound sense of peace on the birth of Christ. The Passion Façade, in stark contrast, depicts the crucifixion and resurrection and arouses strong emotion with its angular forms and harsh lines. Finally, the grandeur Façade, which is currently under construction and will depict the celestial world and the supreme grandeur of God, promises to be an amazing display.

- Grandiosity inside
  You will enter a realm of ethereal splendor as you enter the Sagrada Familia. The intricately vaulted roof, which appears to defy gravity, is supported by soaring columns that resemble towering trees. Every surface

in the interior is illuminated by the play of natural light that filters through the kaleidoscope of stained glass windows, creating a captivating symphony of colors. Everywhere you look, you'll see evidence of Gaud's exquisite attention to detail, including sculptures, mosaics, and floors with intricate patterns that beckon you to explore and find new treasures.

- Religion and symbolism
  The Sagrada Familia is rich in symbolic and spiritual significance in addition to its architectural splendor. Every component of Gaud's basilica was carefully planned to improve the worship experience since he intended it to be a place of worship. The columns, which connect the earth and the sky with their branching forms resembling a dense forest, stand for the connection between nature and the divine. The colorful stained glass windows, which were

painstakingly created in a rainbow of hues, serve as a representation of the diversity and beauty of God's creation. Gaud's profound faith and reverence for the sacred are evident in every design decision and minute detail, which all speak to the divine.

- Go up to greater heights

  The Sagrada Familia gives the chance to ascend its towers and take in stunning panoramic views of Barcelona for the daring and the curious. Enjoy panoramic views of the city skyline, the glistening Mediterranean Sea, and the surrounding area by ascending the spiral stairs that run between the towers. This aerial view provides a singular picture of Gaud's ambition and the enormous scope of the basilica's construction. You will become more and more aware of the meticulous work and enormous effort that went into making this architectural marvel with each step.

- Innovation's driving force

  The Sagrada Familia is a prime example of Gaud's imaginative approach to building, which even now inspires and pushes the envelope. The basilica employs cutting-edge technology and cutting-edge engineering methods despite construction having begun in 1882 and is still ongoing. Gaud's original design is faithfully reproduced while taking into account contemporary improvements thanks to the use of 3D modeling, precise computerized machinery, and extensive structural analysis. Being able to see this ongoing project in progress is proof of the innumerable architects, craftsmen, and artists who have committed their lives to realizing Gaud's ambition.

La Rambla

A dynamic and well-known street throughout the globe, La Rambla is situated in the center of Barcelona. It enthralls both residents and visitors with its distinct appeal and bustling atmosphere as it stretches for 1.2 kilometers from Plaça de Catalunya to the city's shoreline. For anybody visiting Barcelona, La Rambla, also known as Las Ramblas, is a must-visit location because it offers a delightful fusion of history, culture, entertainment, and gastronomy.

As soon as you enter La Rambla, a colorful kaleidoscope of sights, sounds, and smells surrounds you. Numerous businesses, street entertainers, artisans, and flower vendors, as well as a seemingly endless number of cafés and restaurants, line the busy street. You are drawn into the dynamic pace by the upbeat atmosphere.

La Rambla's well-known human statues are one of its principal draws. Uncanny stillness and brief bursts of movement are employed by gifted performers who are dressed as mythological animals, historical figures, or humorous characters to captivate onlookers. They are like living works of art to watch, and it's difficult to resist putting a coin in one of their collection boxes as a sign of gratitude.

As you go along La Rambla, you'll be struck by the impressive architecture that lines the boulevard. The Gran Teatre del Liceu and the Palau de la Virreina are two ornate structures that attract your eye and highlight the city's extensive architectural history. Not only are these landmarks visually stunning, but they also play a significant role as cultural and artistic hubs by organizing exhibitions, performances, and events all year long.

The iconic Boqueria Market is another prominent La Rambla destination. An astonishing variety of fresh vegetables, fish, meats, cheeses, and spices can be found at this colorful food market, which is a feast for the senses. As you make your way through the crowded aisles, colors, fragrances, and sensations surround you, giving you a taste of Catalonia's renowned culinary heritage. For foodies, trying out some of the regional specialties or grabbing a quick bite at one of the market's numerous tapas bars is a must.

You'll come across the iconic Font de Canaletes, a stunning fountain with four lions, as you proceed down La Rambla. Anyone who drinks from this fountain, according to local lore, will eventually return to Barcelona. Taking a sip to secure their return to this intriguing city has become customary for tourists.

The famous Christopher Columbus Monument sits towards the end of La Rambla. This imposing monument honors the illustrious explorer and acts as a metaphorical entryway to the sea while standing tall in Port Vell. You can see Barcelona's stunning beauty from a new vantage point by taking a journey on the nearby cable car, which provides amazing panoramic views of the city's coastline.

La Rambla is more than just a boulevard; it is a dynamic, living organism. The atmosphere changes from being charming to becoming much more so when day gives way to night. The street is suddenly bathed in a sea of lights, and the lively hum lasts long into the evening. People are crammed into tapas bars and restaurants eating delectable meals, and street artists take the stage to play for the audience.

La Rambla's main street is only one area worth exploring. You find local treasures and hidden gems as you explore the side streets and little lanes. For those prepared to venture off the beaten road, there are quaint plazas, lovely shops, and cozy cafés.

Gothic Quarter (Barri Gòtic)

In the center of Barcelona, Spain, is the intriguing and charming enclave known as the Gothic Quarter, or Barri Gtic. This region, which is rich in architectural history and steeped in history, captivates visitors with its unique combination of medieval beauty, winding cobblestone lanes, majestic Gothic buildings, and lively atmosphere. The Gothic Quarter is a must-visit location for anyone looking to get a true sense of Barcelona thanks to its distinctive attractions and entertaining activities.

You are immediately transported back in time as soon as you enter the Gothic Quarter. You are invited to explore the nearly 2,000-year-old labyrinthine streets and learn their secrets. Spend some time wandering through the narrow lanes that are lined with beautiful buildings, secret plazas, and welcoming cafes. The streets are alive with people and visitors alike, weaving through them to create a vivid tapestry of sights, sounds, and smells.

The majestic Barcelona Cathedral, often referred to as the Cathedral of the Holy Cross and Saint Eulalia, is one of the most well-known sights in the Gothic Quarter. With its towering spires, elaborate facades, and breathtaking stained glass windows, this magnificent work of Gothic architecture mesmerizes tourists. Enter the cathedral, take in the peaceful atmosphere, and admire the complex aspects of the interior, such as the lovely cloister and the crypt where Saint Eulalia is interred.

The Plaça del Rei, a large square rich in history, may be found if you delve even deeper into the area. The Palau Reial Major, the former royal residence of the Counts of Barcelona, is located here. Discover the lavish rooms and the fascinating museum located within, which displays Roman ruins and medieval items, offering a peek into the city's past.

Visit the charming Plaça Sant Felip Neri, a tiny square tucked away from the busy people, as you proceed through the Gothic Quarter. A gorgeous fountain and lovely structures line the perimeter of this serene paradise. The church's walls still bear the scars of the Spanish Civil War, which serve as a melancholy reminder of the city's turbulent past.

Without taking advantage of its thriving culinary scene, one cannot truly explore the Gothic Quarter. The area is teeming with modern eateries, charming cafes, and traditional tapas bars. A delicious selection of Spanish treats, from scrumptious patatas bravas to succulent jamón ibérico, can be enjoyed if you find a nice location in a hidden corner. The culinary treats of the Gothic Quarter will leave you wanting more.

The Gothic Quarter becomes a completely different environment once twilight falls. As locals and tourists throng to the area's vibrant pubs and clubs, the small streets come alive with an intoxicating energy. Discover a hip cocktail bar or a classic tavern, then let the vibrant nightlife take you by surprise. You may be sure that you'll enjoy a fun-filled evening thanks to the thrilling ambiance and the welcoming people.

The Gothic Quarter provides a treasure trove of boutique shops, artisanal products, and eccentric galleries in addition to its architectural treasures and lively atmosphere. Take a stroll through Carrer dels Banys Nous, a lovely street lined with specialized stores and antique stores. Discover one-of-a-kind keepsakes, fashionable clothing, and intriguing artwork, each with a unique tale to tell.

Join one of the numerous walking tours offered to get the full feel of the Gothic Quarter. You will be led by knowledgeable guides through the confusing streets, who will reveal hidden treasures and regale you with fascinating tales and legends. These guided tours provide a greater understanding of the neighborhood's rich cultural legacy, whether they are ghost tours, historical explorations, or gastronomic excursions.

Barceloneta Beach

A colorful and alluring location, Barcelona's Barceloneta Beach easily combines the beauty of the Mediterranean Sea with a buzzing and upbeat environment. Both locals and visitors are drawn in by its magnetic attractiveness, which draws them to a variety of attractions and a lively atmosphere that makes an impression. Barceloneta Beach is a heavenly refuge that perfectly captures Barcelona's beach culture with its golden sands, clean waves, and variety of leisure activities.

Your senses are immediately heightened as soon as you step onto the beach by the sea's salty aroma and the soothing caress of the coastal breeze. You may appreciate the warmth and beauty of the beach as it stretches out in front of you. The golden sand glistens in the sunlight and begs you to take off your shoes and bury your toes in its gentle grains. The rhythmic sound of the waves breaking along the shore provides a calming symphony that calms your thoughts and takes you to a serene location as you stroll along the shore.

A colorful tapestry of cultures and languages is created at Barceloneta Beach by the confluence of people from all walks of life. As you observe families having picnics, friendship groups having animated chats, and people finding respite in quiet settings, it truly captures the multicultural character of Barcelona. People play beach volleyball, sail kites, or just relax under bright parasols while soaking up the warmth of the Mediterranean sun. The atmosphere is filled with joy and laughter.

Barceloneta Beach is a water sports enthusiast's dream come true. Activities like windsurfing, paddleboarding, and kayaking may all be done on the clear waters. To add even more excitement to their beach excursions, thrill-seekers can also partake in thrilling activities like jet skiing or parasailing. There are lots of boat tours that let you explore the coastline and take in panoramic views of the city from the water if you're looking for a more laid-back aquatic experience.

In addition to the sand and water, Barceloneta Beach provides a wide variety of culinary treats that will tempt your palate. The promenade is lined with chiringuitos (beach bars) and restaurants that face the beach and serve a tempting array of seafood specialties, tapas, and cool drinks. You can take in the energetic environment while enjoying a plate of freshly caught paella or sipping a cool sangria.

The seaside promenade is a bustling, vibrant scene in and of itself. Along its length, you can find merchants selling their wares, street entertainers, and artists. As you take a stroll, the sound of music fills the air as superb musicians create a lovely background. A variety of beachwear, trinkets, and regional crafts are available from the quaint shops and boutiques along the promenade. Finding a special souvenir to remember your trip couldn't be easier.

In addition to the beach, Barceloneta is conveniently situated close to many other Barcelona attractions. The neighborhood itself emanates a particular personality thanks to its winding alleyways, endearing squares, and lively tapas bars. A short stroll will take you to the well-known Port Vell, a bustling harbor dotted with opulent ships, hip bars, and a wide range of entertainment alternatives. The captivating Gothic Quarter and Antoni Gaud's architectural wonders, such as the Sagrada Familia and Park Güell, are just a little further away and are ready for your investigation.

Barceloneta Beach captures the spirit of Barcelona's joie de vivre by providing a fascinating fusion of scenic views, fun activities, and a buzzing atmosphere. It is a location where the city's essence genuinely comes to life, enticing everyone who comes there with its contagious attitude and welcoming embrace of the Mediterranean. Whether you're looking for adventure, relaxation, or just a memorable day by the sea, Barceloneta Beach guarantees an outstanding experience that will make you want to go back and experience its allure once more.

Chapter 4

Exploring Barcelona Neighborhoods

El Born

In the center of Barcelona, Spain, is a bustling district called El Born. El Born offers a remarkable experience that skillfully combines the ancient and the new thanks to its crooked, twisting alleyways, historical sites, and bustling ambiance. Here is a snapshot of what El Born has to offer in terms of fun and excitement, from its fascinating history to its vibrant nightlife.

The distinctive architecture of El Born is one of the first things that draw your notice. Numerous medieval structures that have been wonderfully preserved and are decorated with exquisite features and vivid colors can be found in the area. As you stroll through the streets, you'll have a sense of being transported back in time as you take in the striking facades and secret courtyards that reveal the history of the city.

Unquestionably, the iconic Mercat del Born, a spectacular iron-framed market from the late 19th century, is the center of El Born. El Born Centre de Cultura i Memoria is the name given to the building's current incarnation as a cultural hub. This stunning piece of architecture serves as a focal point for displays, performances, and other activities honoring Barcelona's past and present. It's like going on an archaeological adventure to explore the market's underground ruins, which protect the remains of the medieval city.

El Born is recognized for having a creative spirit. The area is home to a large number of galleries, shops, and workshops that feature the work of regional designers and artists. You can lose hours browsing the unusual collection of modern art, clothing, and crafts, picking up one-of-a-kind gifts for loved ones back home, or just taking in the area's creative atmosphere.

El Born has a tempting variety of culinary pleasures to choose from. There is something for every pallet, from classic tapas bars to cutting-edge restaurants. Eat delicious food while relaxing with a drink of local wine or a crisp craft beer at one of the sidewalk cafés. With its inventive fusion cuisine and emphasis on local, fresh ingredients, the neighborhood's food culture fully captures Barcelona's culinary prowess.

El Born becomes a hopping nightlife area as soon as the sun goes down. Locals and visitors alike throng to the area's bars and clubs, creating a vibrant atmosphere. There is a location to suit every taste, from quaint, back-alley bars to swanky cocktail lounges. El Born provides a diverse and active nightlife culture that caters to everyone, whether you prefer to sip on beautifully prepared drinks, dance to the beat of live music, or have stimulating chats with new acquaintances.

El Born offers a wide range of cultural events all year long in addition to its architectural and culinary attractions. Concerts, festivals, and street performances that highlight the thriving local arts scene fill the neighborhood's plazas and parks. There's always something going on at El Born that will excite and inspire you, from flamenco performances to open-air movie screenings.

In addition to its urban appeal, El Born is ideally placed close to some of Barcelona's most well-known sites. You may rest amidst lush vegetation, rent a boat, or visit the Barcelona Zoo in the charming Ciutadella Park, which is only a short stroll away. You may locate the breathtaking Gothic Quarter nearby, which is home to winding alleyways, imposing cathedrals, and attractive squares. A nice break from the hectic daily life may be found at the beach, which is also easily accessible.

El Raval

In the center of Barcelona, Spain, is a thriving area called El Raval. El Raval has gained popularity as a travel destination for both locals and tourists due to its extensive history, rich cultural diversity, and renowned for its buzzing atmosphere. With a focus on El Raval's history, cultural significance, architecture, and current developments, this essay will examine the distinctive features and attractions of the neighborhood.

El Raval's history begins in the Middle Ages when it was first developed as one of the earliest suburbs outside the city walls. It has seen numerous changes over the years, developing into the vibrant and diversified neighborhood we see today. Historically, El Raval was known for having a working-class population and for having a bad reputation for poverty and crime. It has become a multicultural and creative hotspot, meanwhile, as a result of substantial restoration initiatives in recent years.

Numerous sights and attractions can be found in the neighborhood. La Rambla, a well-known street that runs through El Raval, is one of the most notable locations. La Rambla has a bustling ambiance because it is lined with cafes, stores, street entertainers, and market booths. It serves as a bustling gathering spot and a vivid representation of Barcelona's multicultural nature.

El Raval also has a rich architectural history. The area is a fusion of the ancient and the new, with both medieval and contemporary architecture. The Hospital de la Santa Creu I Sant Pau, a beautiful modernist structure created by Llus Domènech I Montaner, is one of the area's architectural highlights. Another interesting building is the Palau Güell, a residence created by renowned architect

Antoni Gaud. The inventiveness and invention that Barcelona is renowned for are on display in these architectural wonders.

El Raval is well-known for its cultural institutions in addition to its amazing architecture. An excellent collection of contemporary art is kept in the Museum of Contemporary Art of Barcelona (MACBA), a well-known cultural institution. It attracts art fans from all over the world by functioning as a venue for exhibitions, performances, and cultural activities. The Centre de Cultura Contemporània de Barcelona (CCCB), a hub for contemporary culture, promotes it through a variety of exhibitions, discussions, and multimedia works.

El Raval is renowned for its varied and energetic gastronomic scene. The area is home to a large number of eateries, cafes, and pubs that serve a variety of cuisines to satisfy every preference. El Raval offers a variety of delectable food options, from traditional Catalan dishes to worldwide fusion dishes. Visitors can indulge in tapas, seafood, and other gastronomic delights while exploring the neighborhood's winding lanes.

El Raval is a neighborhood that is still developing in addition to its historical and cultural highlights. The advent of inventive companies, co-working spaces, and creative businesses in recent years has helped the area change into a hotbed of entrepreneurship and innovation. Due to the abundance of galleries, studios, and music venues that line the streets, the area has also grown to be a hub for musicians, designers, and artists.

El Raval hasn't lost any of its character or sense of neighborhood despite its makeover. The area has succeeded in striking a balance between upholding its history and embracing modernity, resulting in a distinctive ambiance that is both lively and hospitable. El Raval is an intriguing and alluring place for anyone looking for an immersive experience in the heart of Barcelona thanks to this fusion of heritage and modernity.

Poble Sec

In the Spanish city of Barcelona, Poble Sec is a thriving area. Known for its distinctive fusion of historical charm, cultural diversity, and artistic flair, it is located on the slopes of Montjuic Hill. Poble Sec provides a captivating experience for both residents and visitors thanks to its rich history, diversified population, and variety of activities.

Poble Sec's history dates back to the 19th century, a time of substantial urban expansion in the area. It began as an industrial region before transitioning into a working-class neighborhood and drawing a diverse population of people. Poble Sec has developed into a vibrant and international neighborhood throughout the years.

Poble Sec's distinctive architectural design is one of its most noticeable characteristics. Many of the stunning structures that line the streets were constructed during the Modernist era and have elaborate facades and ornamental embellishments. The neighborhood's distinctive character is enhanced by these architectural marvels, which also serve as a reminder of the area's rich past.

Poble Sec has a thriving arts community as well. The iconic El Molino, a venerable cabaret theater that has been delighting audiences since 1898, is one of many theaters in the region. El Molino, a landmark of Barcelona's nightlife, is known for its risqué performances.

The Museum of Catalan Ethnology, which sheds light on the regional traditions and customs of Catalonia, is another cultural gem in Poble Sec. The museum contains a collection of items and displays that highlight the region's rich cultural past.

Poble Sec offers a wide range of culinary delights in addition to its cultural attractions. The area is well-known for its tapas bars and traditional Catalan restaurants, where guests may indulge in a selection of regional fare. Poble Sec offers a wide variety of delectable foods, such as paella, shellfish, pintxos, and vermouth.

Poble Sec is ideally situated to begin visiting Barcelona's other attractions because of its central location. Montjuc, a notable hill with beautiful views of the city, is nearby and only a short stroll away. The Montjuic Castle, the Magic Fountain of Montjuic, and the Olympic Stadium are just a few of the famous sites that can be seen in Montjuic.

Additionally, Poble Sec has excellent access to other parts of Barcelona via bus and metro lines. As a result, it is simple for locals and tourists to explore other areas of the city, such as the well-known La Rambla, the Gothic Quarter, and the famed Sagrada Familia.

Poble Sec is a neighborhood that nurtures a strong sense of community in addition to its historical and cultural attractions. Local markets, cafes, and stores line the streets, attracting locals who congregate there to socialize. The neighborhood's vibrant energy and warm heartedness foster a sense of community and make it a welcoming location to live or visit.

Barceloneta

Barcelona, Catalonia, Spain's metropolis of Barcelona is home to the thriving neighborhood of Barceloneta. Because of its location on the eastern end of the city's shoreline, it is a well-liked vacation spot for both locals and visitors who are drawn to its stunning beaches, vibrant environment, and rich cultural legacy. Barceloneta, a neighborhood with a long history that offers a distinctive fusion of tradition and modernity, has grown from a sleepy fishing town to a vibrant and active neighborhood.

To accommodate the expanding number of fishermen who relied on the sea for their livelihoods, Barceloneta was first developed in the 18th century. Visitors can get a look into the neighborhood's past thanks to the small streets and low-rise buildings in Barceloneta, which still attest to its modest beginnings. The neighborhood's name, which translates to "little Barcelona" in Catalan, expresses the area's unique character within the city.

Barceloneta's long, sandy beach, which hugs the Mediterranean coastline, is one of the city's main draws. The beachfront is the center of activity, especially in the summer when both locals and visitors throng to its banks to bask in the sun, bathe in the cool seas, or partake in water sports. The beach is bordered by a variety of eateries, cafes, and bars that serve a variety of eats and drinks. Traditional seafood dishes, tapas, or just a refreshing beverage can be enjoyed by guests as they take in the mesmerizing sea views.

In addition to its beach, Barceloneta is renowned for its distinctive architectural design. The tiny, brightly colored buildings that make up the majority of the area often have balconies and rooftop terraces. These buildings produce a distinct aesthetic and add to the area's lively vibe. You may find neighborhood stores, boutiques, and markets on the streets where you can get genuine Catalan goods and crafts. Barceloneta is also the location of the renowned Mercat de la Barceloneta, a lively food market where you can discover a variety of fresh produce, fish, and other gastronomic pleasures.

Barceloneta has several noteworthy landmarks and attractions for people who are interested in the history and culture of the area. The Sant Miquel del Port church, an exquisite example of Gothic architecture from the 18th century, is one such landmark. For lovers of architecture and history, the church is a must-visit location because of its exquisite interior design and detailed features. The Museu d'Història de Barcelona (Barcelona History Museum) is another noteworthy location. It covers the history of the city through a variety of exhibits and artifacts and offers insightful information about the development of Barceloneta and its significance in Barcelona's past.

Barceloneta is closely associated with sports in general, but sailing and water sports in particular. The sailing competitions at the 1992 Summer Olympics were held at Port Olympic, which is located in the neighborhood. The port is still a busy marina today, with yachts, boats, and restaurants by the sea. Visitors can take a stroll down the promenade, gaze at the impressive ships, or even hire a boat to tour the nearby shoreline.

Barceloneta has daytime attractions as well as a vibrant nightlife scene that comes to life at night.

The area is home to a wide range of taverns, clubs, and music venues that accommodate all interests and preferences. Whether you're looking for a night of dancing to the hottest sounds or a calm cocktail by the beach, Barceloneta has a wide variety of possibilities.

Sarrià-Sant Gervasi

The lovely neighborhood of Sarrià-Sant Gervasi is situated in the northern region of Barcelona, Catalonia, Spain. Sarrià-Sant Gervasi offers a distinctive fusion of modernity and history and is well known for its upmarket residential districts, historical landmarks, and thriving cultural environment. The area has gained popularity as a travel destination for both locals and tourists because of its extensive attractions and rich history.

Sarrià and Sant Gervasi de Cassoles, the two original municipalities that made up Sarrià-Sant Gervasi, were combined into one in 1897. Due to the district's preservation of its original identity, its streets, historic structures, and lovely parks are in excellent condition. One of Barcelona's wealthiest neighborhoods, it is frequently characterized as.

Sarrià-Sant Gervasi's lovely village-like environment is one of its key attractions. A lively and pleasant atmosphere is created by the streets' abundance of chic stores, hip cafes, and neighborhood shops. Numerous architectural treasures, including modernist structures created by well-known architects like Josep Puig I Cadafalch and Antoni Gaud, can also be seen in the neighborhood.

The renowned Parc de Collserola is a must-see attraction in Sarrià-Sant Gervasi. With a total size of more than 8,000 hectares, this vast natural park provides stunning vistas of Barcelona and its surroundings. It's the perfect location for outdoor pursuits like riding, hiking, and picnics since it lets people get away from the bustle of the city and experience nature.

CosmoCaixa Barcelona, a science museum that provides an engaging trip through many scientific disciplines, is another noteworthy attraction in the neighborhood. The museum offers an entertaining and instructive experience for visitors of all ages with interactive displays, a planetarium, and a rainforest simulation.

Several significant cultural institutions are located in Sarrià-Sant Gervasi. While the Museu dels Automats hosts a one-of-a-kind exhibition of robotic toys and figurines, the Galeria Mayoral exhibits an amazing selection of contemporary art. Additionally, the area holds several festivals and cultural occasions all year long, such as the Sant Medir Festival and the Sarrià Festivities, which honor regional traditions and customs.

Sarrià-Sant Gervasi has a wide selection of top-notch restaurants and taverns for people looking for a taste of authentic Catalan cuisine. The district's dining establishments offer mouthwatering tapas, fresh seafood, and regional specialties to patrons while they take in the cozy and welcoming ambiance.

Additionally, the area has a lot of green areas where people may unwind and enjoy. The Turó Park offers a pleasant haven in the middle of the city with its beautiful gardens and calming ponds. Another lovely park, the Gardens of Doctor Pla I Armengol, provides a gorgeous backdrop for strolls or peaceful times of contemplation.

With numerous metro and bus lines linking Sarrià-Sant Gervasi to the rest of Barcelona, transportation is simple and convenient. As a result, tourists will find it simple to explore other well-known sights in the city, such as Park Güell and the renowned Sagrada Famlia, which are both conveniently close by.

Chapter 5

Museums and Galleries

Picasso Museum

A renowned organization dedicated to Pablo Picasso's life and artistic output is the Picasso Museum in Barcelona. Picasso's vast body of work is displayed in this museum, which is housed in five opulent medieval palaces and is located in the city's Gothic Quarter. The museum offers visitors an unrivaled chance to examine the development of Picasso's artistic career because of its extensive history and a wide variety of masterpieces.

Jaume Sabartés, Picasso's friend and secretary, worked hard to get the museum open to the public in 1963. Sabartés had a key role in obtaining various gifts from Picasso's private collection, assuring that the museum would develop into a thorough archive of his work. Over 4,200 pieces of art from the artist's complete body of work, including paintings, sculptures, ceramics, sketches, and engravings, are housed in the museum's collection.

The early works collection, which offers insight into Picasso's formative years as an artist, is one of the centerpieces of the museum. From the Blue Period to the Rose Period, visitors can see how his early experiments and various inspirations influenced his artistic style. This period produced notable works including "Science and Charity" and "The Madman."

Picasso co-founded the revolutionary creative movement known as the Cubists, and the museum's collection includes a sizable number of his iconic Cubist pieces. The artist's innovative use of fragmented forms and many angles to represent reality is on display for everyone to see. Les

Demoiselles d'Avignon and "Woman with a Guitar" are two important examples of his Cubist paintings.

Picasso's sculptures are shown around the museum together with his paintings. Visitors can feel these three-dimensional works, which allows them to better understand Picasso's mastery of many mediums and methods. A couple of notable sculptures include "The Glass of Absinthe" and "Head of a Woman."

Picasso's life and artistic growth are completely explored in the museum's display areas, which have been thoughtfully organized. The design guarantees a chronological investigation of his work, enabling visitors to follow his artistic development from his formative years in Barcelona to his later international fame. To offer new viewpoints and deeper insights into Picasso's art, the museum also organizes transient exhibitions that delve further into particular subjects or eras of his career.

In addition to the artwork, the museum is aesthetically pleasing. The collection is housed in a network of palaces that are connected by grand staircases and Gothic courtyards, which add to the overall mood. The museum's restoration works have maintained the historical integrity of the structures, resulting in a seamless fusion of old-world charm and appreciation for contemporary art.

The museum also has a library and a study center for individuals looking to learn more about Picasso's influences and creative process. A comprehensive library of books, catalogs, and archives about Picasso's life and works is available to researchers and art fans.

The Picasso Museum in Barcelona is more than simply a destination for art lovers; it offers an immersive experience that enables guests to enter the universe of the artist. For visitors of all ages, the museum offers guided tours, workshops, and educational programs that promote participation and active engagement. Everyone may understand and engage with Picasso's legacy because of the museum's dedication to accessibility, regardless of their background or prior knowledge of art.

Museu Nacional d'Art de Catalunya

An extensive collection of Catalan artwork from many eras is on display at the Museu Nacional d'Art de Catalunya (MNAC) in Barcelona, a renowned cultural center. It is one of the most significant museums in the area, drawing visitors and residents alike with its extensive collection of artwork and historical relevance. The MNAC is a landmark of Catalan culture and artistic expression due to its stunning location atop Montjuc Hill and its century-long existence.

The museum has its roots in the late 19th century when Barcelona attempted to establish a location devoted to promoting and preserving Catalan art. The museum's long-term residence is the Palau Nacional, a grandiose palace built for the 1929 International Exposition. The museum is even more spectacular and alluring because of its magnificent architecture, which has a large, dominating central dome.

The extensive collection of the MNAC features works in a variety of artistic mediums, such as painting, sculpture, drawing, photography, and decorative arts. Visitors can see pieces of art that range in time from the Romanesque era to the 20th century, offering a thorough picture of Catalan artistic development. The Romanesque collection stands out because it contains one of the largest and most significant collections of works in this style anywhere in the world.

As visitors explore the museum's halls, they come across works of art by well-known Catalan creators including Ramon Casas, Santiago Rusiol, and

Joaquim Mir, who had a significant impact on the Modernisme movement. The Modernisme collection features the distinctive Catalan art nouveau movement, which is distinguished by its decorative embellishments and incorporation of natural elements into artistic representations.

The MNAC also has a sizable collection of Gothic artwork, which includes beautiful altarpieces, sculptures, and paintings. By spotlighting the creative accomplishments of individuals like Jaume Huguet and Pere Serra, this book reflects the spirit of Catalonia's Gothic era. A collection of Renaissance and Baroque art is also on display in the museum, including pieces by Rubens, Velázquez, and El Greco.

In addition to its permanent collections, the MNAC frequently offers temporary exhibitions, guaranteeing visitors a vibrant and constantly-evolving experience. A deeper investigation of diverse artistic trends and historical settings is provided by these exhibitions, which frequently concentrate on certain themes or individuals.

The museum's position, which offers breathtaking panoramic views of Barcelona, is unquestionably one of its attractions. Visitors may take in the city's skyline, which features famous structures like the Sagrada Familia and Montjuic Castle, from the roomy terrace next to the Palau Nacional. The stunning view perfectly complements the aesthetic trip inside the museum, enriching the experience as a whole.

The MNAC uses cutting-edge technology and multimedia resources to improve visitor engagement and comprehension. Visitors can learn more about the artworks and the history behind them by using interactive touch screens, audio guides, and virtual reality experiences. These cutting-edge tools enable a more engaging and instructive museum experience for everyone.

The MNAC acts as a center for research and education in addition to providing artistic activities. The building is home to a specialist library and documentation center that facilitates academic endeavors and provides tools for students, researchers, and art historians. Conferences, talks, and workshops are held at the museum, further enhancing Barcelona's cultural and intellectual climate.

The Museu Nacional d'Art de Catalunya has established itself as a key player in Barcelona's cultural landscape, drawing art lovers, history fans, and curious tourists alike. For those seeking a greater understanding of Catalan art and culture, its broad collection, magnificent setting, and dedication to education make it a must-visit venue. The MNAC is a key player in safeguarding and promoting Catalonia's rich artistic tradition and working as a custodian of the region's cultural legacy, ensuring its survival for future generations.

Joan Miró Foundation

In Barcelona, Spain, there is a prominent museum called the Joan Miró Foundation that is devoted to the works and life of the Catalan artist Joan Miró. The foundation, which was started in 1975, has a significant place in the art world and welcomes a lot of tourists from all over the world who come to admire Miró's singular aesthetic perspective.

Josep Llus Sert, a close friend of Miró, created the foundation's edifice, which is itself a work of art in architecture. Combining elements of usefulness and aesthetics, the building merges in perfectly with the surrounding environment. The room's spaciousness and inviting mood go well with the artist's vivid and imaginative creations. Its white walls and huge windows provide this.

The collection of the foundation includes a wide variety of Miró's works, including drawings, paintings, sculptures, textiles, and ceramics. These works, which cover many phases of Miró's career, show how the artist has developed over time and has experimented with a wide range of mediums. The collection showcases lesser-known works that provide light on Miró's creative process in addition to his renowned paintings that have come to represent him.

One of the foundation's centerpieces is the "Miró's Studio," which has been meticulously reconstructed to mimic the artist's original workshop. Visitors can enter Miró's universe and become surrounded by his easels, brushes, and other art supplies, learning more about his creative process and the surroundings that inspired it. The artist's studio offers a rare window into his or her creative process as well as an opportunity to feel close to the artist, Miró.

In addition to its permanent collection, the foundation often holds temporary exhibitions that include pieces by other contemporary artists, completing Miró's body of work and offering a broader view of modern art. The subjects covered in these shows frequently touch on Miró's artistic influences, the social setting in which he produced his work, or current cultural movements that share his aesthetic sensibilities. The foundation will continue to be a lively and interesting location for art fans of all kinds thanks to this innovative approach.

The Joan Miró Foundation provides a range of cultural and educational programs in addition to its exhibition spaces. For guests of all ages, these include seminars, talks, tours, and educational activities. The mission of the foundation is to encourage visitors to have a strong appreciation for Miró's work as well as to be creative and to discover their artistic potential.

The foundation's dedication to protecting and promoting Miró's artistic heritage goes beyond the confines of the museum. It actively cooperates with various cultural organizations all around the world, lending its artworks for exhibitions and facilitating the interchange of information and ideas. By doing this, the foundation makes certain that Miró's artwork remains accessible to a large audience worldwide and adds to the conversation about modern and contemporary art as a whole.

The Joan Miró Foundation has developed into not just an important cultural organization in Barcelona but also a representation of the artistic legacy of the city. Visitors may see amazing panoramic views of Barcelona thanks to its well-chosen location on Montjuc, a hill above the city, which adds to the total enjoyment. Because of the foundation's dedication to artistic excellence, community engagement, and the preservation of Miró's legacy, it is now well recognized as a must-visit location for both art lovers and culture vultures.

Barcelona Museum of Contemporary Art

Located in the center of Barcelona, Spain, the Barcelona Museum of Contemporary Art (MACBA) is a prominent cultural facility. The museum, created by renowned American architect Richard Meier, is a defining example of the city's modern art and architecture. Since its founding in 1995, the MACBA has been instrumental in displaying and advancing contemporary art from Catalonia and other parts of the world.

The MACBA building is a stunning illustration of modernist architecture, located in the thriving El Raval area. It contrasts nicely with the nearby old structures thanks to its stark white facade, which is made up of geometric shapes and straight lines. The museum, which is more than 14,000 square meters in size, is home to a sizable collection of modern works of art from the second half of the 20th century to the present.

The permanent collection at the MACBA contains more than 5,000 works of art in a variety of media, including painting, sculpture, photography, video art, and installations. Artistic movements like abstract expressionism, pop art, minimalism, conceptual art, and the avant-garde are emphasized by the museum's curators. Through its carefully planned exhibitions, the MACBA aims to showcase the global range of contemporary art while placing a focus on Spanish and Catalan artists.

The museum's commitment to promoting multidisciplinary dialogue and critical thinking is one of its best features. Visitors of all ages are interested in the conferences, workshops, and educational activities that MACBA frequently offers. These programs encourage discussion between artists, curators, academics, and the general public to advance a deeper knowledge of contemporary art. The museum's dedication to outreach and education highlights its function as an active cultural center within Barcelona's artistic community.

Visitors can enjoy a dynamic and ever-changing artistic experience thanks to the MACBA's exhibition program, which is always expanding. To give both up-and-coming and established artists a stage, the museum frequently hosts solo exhibitions by renowned contemporary artists. Ongoing social, political, and environmental themes are examined via art in its thematic group shows. The MACBA aims to question established conventions and promote public conversation by showcasing a wide spectrum of artistic ideas.

Through digital media, the MACBA expands its reach beyond its physical locations and opens up art to a larger audience. Visitors can interact with art remotely thanks to the museum's website's virtual exhibitions, online collections, and interactive tools. By bridging the gap between the actual and virtual worlds of art appreciation, this digital presence strengthens the MACBA's dedication to diversity and cross-cultural dialogue.

In addition to being a venue for exhibitions, the MACBA is an important location for both study and preservation. Its library and archive have a substantial collection of books, catalogs, periodicals, and multimedia materials, making it a priceless tool for academics, students, and art fans. By working with academic institutions and other cultural organizations, the museum actively contributes to the study of art history and advances our understanding of contemporary art.

The MACBA presents a range of cultural events, such as film screenings, performances, and concerts, in addition to its permanent collection and short-term exhibitions. By providing a lively and interesting environment for visitors, these diverse activities further enhance the museum experience.

The Barcelona Museum of Contemporary Art has solidified its reputation as a progressive organization that honors and promotes the variety of contemporary art. The MACBA continues to influence Barcelona's cultural scene and invigorate a large audience thanks to its stunning architectural design, cutting-edge exhibitions, educational programs, and digital projects. Whether you are an art enthusiast, a curious visitor, or a lifelong learner, a trip to the MACBA is a rewarding experience that takes you on a fascinating journey through the complexity and beauties of contemporary art.

Maritime Museum of Barcelona

A remarkable institution, the Maritime Museum of Barcelona takes visitors on a fascinating tour through the city's and the Mediterranean region's maritime heritage and history. The museum, which is situated in the center of Barcelona, Spain, pays homage to the city's vibrant nautical history by presenting a variety of antiques, exhibitions, and interactive displays that provide visitors with an engaging experience.

The museum is located in the venerable Royal Shipyards of Barcelona or Drassanes Reials de Barcelona in Catalan. These 13th-century shipyards were once the hub of Barcelona's naval industry and were crucial to the city's nautical dominance during the Middle Ages and Early Modern Periods. The structures themselves are magnificent examples of Gothic architecture, and their commanding presence enhances the attraction of the museum.

Visitors are welcomed to the Nautical Museum with a sizable collection of displays that explore all facets of nautical history. Themed displays allow visitors to the museum to examine various aspects of nautical life, including shipbuilding, navigation, exploration, trade, and naval combat. Through intricate models, relics, documents, and multimedia presentations, the displays are painstakingly selected and provide a wealth of information.

The museum's enormous collection of model ships is one of its best features. These finely detailed reproductions offer a window into how ship design and building have changed over time. The models represent the various kinds of ships that have traveled the Mediterranean Sea throughout history, from ancient Mediterranean vessels to majestic galleons and sleek modern ships. Visitors can be in awe of the artistry and educate themselves on the technological innovations that transformed maritime transportation.

Additionally, a noteworthy collection of historical relics, such as weapons, navigational tools, and explorers' and sailors' personal effects are kept at the museum. These relics provide a concrete link to the past and give visitors a better understanding of the struggles and everyday experiences of mariners throughout history. The use of interactive displays enables visitors to interact with the exhibits and learn more about the nautical industry.

The Marine Museum of Barcelona also offers transient exhibitions that focus on certain subjects associated with marine history, culture, and adventure. Even for frequent visitors, these exhibitions provide different subjects with a new perspective and make sure there is always something new to learn at the museum.

For guests of all ages, the museum also provides educational activities and programs. Visitors can take part in workshops, tours, and interactive activities as part of these programs, which are designed to give them a hands-on learning experience. The museum hopes to spread knowledge about maritime heritage and the significance of the sea in forming Barcelona's history and identity as well as that of the Mediterranean area through these activities.

The Barcelona Maritime Museum is a thriving cultural hub in addition to a site for historical inquiry. To study and commemorate maritime heritage, the museum conducts lectures, conferences, and other cultural activities. It acts as a center for study and cooperation, promoting a better comprehension of the maritime world and its importance in modern society.

Chapter 6

Parks and Gardens

Park Güell

In the center of Barcelona, Spain, stands Park Güell, a colorful and fantastical work of art. This magnificent park was created by the well-known architect Antoni Gaud and serves as a tribute to both the elegance of Catalan modernism and his singular aesthetic vision. The immersive experience that Park Güell offers visitors is both entertaining and inspiring because of its vivid colors, organic shapes, and whimsical features.

As soon as you enter the park, you are met by a great staircase decorated with the "Salvador Dragon," a mosaic dragon. The whimsical and imaginative atmosphere that awaits visitors to the park is set by this charming creature, which is coated in vibrant tiles. Because it is believed that the dragon will bring luck, tourists frequently assemble around it to take pictures and make wishes.

As you stroll through the park, you'll come across a plethora of colorful and whimsical mosaic sculptures, seats, and walkways that were all painstakingly made by Gaud and his team. Breaking ceramic tiles and arranging them in complex patterns is a mosaic technique known as "trends." As a result, there is a stunning display of hues and textures that seem to come to life as the sun dances across them.

The Hypostyle Room, a sizable terrace supported by 86 Doric columns, is among the most well-known aspects of the park. A magnificent forest-like ambiance is created by the columns, which resemble tall palm trees. As you look around the room, you'll see that the ceiling is decorated with a lovely canopy of mosaic tiles in an erratic pattern.

Visitors are invited to be in awe and wonder at Gaud's brilliance in this exceptional architectural masterpiece.

The famous main terrace, also referred to as the "Greek Theatre," is one of Park Güell's highlights. The Mediterranean Sea and Barcelona's skyline are both visible from this large area in all directions. The patio has a long, curved bench surrounding it that is decorated with colorful mosaic tiles, making it the ideal place to rest, unwind, and take in the breathtaking surroundings. Visitors frequently congregate there to socialize, snap photos, and take spectacular views.

Park Güell is home to stunning landscapes and open areas in addition to its architectural marvels. The landscaping of the park harmoniously combines with Gaud's architecture to produce a harmonic synthesis of art and nature. You'll come across rich greenery, including palm trees, cypress trees, and numerous flowering species, as you stroll along the twisting walkways. It is the perfect location to get away from the busy city and reconnect with nature because of the pleasant scents and peaceful atmosphere.

Park Güell offers a variety of leisure opportunities for visitors of all ages in addition to its scenic treats. There are open areas in the park where people can picnic, play games, or just enjoy the sunshine. Children will delight in the play areas, which were created with inventive and vibrant components that drew inspiration from Gaud's designs. Additionally, the park holds concerts, exhibitions, and cultural events, which enhances the lively mood.

A trip to Park Güell is a memorable experience that transcends age and time. Whether you're a fan of architecture, appreciate art, or are just looking for a place to unwind, the park provides a wonderful respite. It encourages wonder and imagination, and it offers a chance to become fully immersed in Antoni Gaud's genius.

You can experience Gaud's fun and imaginative attitude as you stroll through the park's magical settings. A whimsical and peaceful environment is created by the union of vivid hues, organic shapes, and minute details. Park Güell is an example of the transformative power of art and imagination, and it perfectly reflects the essence of Barcelona's rich cultural past.

Montjuïc Park

A variety of thrilling experiences are available for guests of all ages at Barcelona's Montjuc Park, a lively and captivating location. This huge park is a veritable playground for adventure and enjoyment, offering breathtaking views of the city, cultural attractions, lush gardens, and recreational pursuits.

The stunning Montjuc Castle, towering atop the hill, greets you as you enter Montjuc Park. The castle, which was once constructed as a military stronghold, provides an intriguing look into Barcelona's past. Admire the breathtaking views of the city and the Mediterranean Sea while exploring its historic walls and ramparts. Additionally, the castle organizes several exhibitions and events all year long, which increases its appeal.

Several exquisitely planted gardens may be found throughout the park as you make your way down from the castle. The vivid variety of succulents and cacti at the Jardins de Mossèn Cinto Verdaguer, which is a must-see, is stunning. Laribal's tiered gardens, with their cascading fountains, decorative ponds, and vibrant flora, provide a peaceful setting for reflection and relaxation. With its imaginative sculptures, the Jardins de Joan Brossa will pique your curiosity.

The renowned Montjuc Magic Fountain is one of the park's features. It's a great show to watch this magnificent display of water, music, and light. As dusk falls, the fountain awakens, entrancing onlookers with its synchronized water jets and a symphony of colors. You can encounter a mesmerizing experience that will leave you enthralled at the Magic Fountain shows, which are free to attend and happen frequently.

Numerous renowned museums and cultural institutions may be found in Montjuc Park for art lovers. A wide variety of Catalan artwork, from Romanesque classics to modernist pieces, is on display in the Museu Nacional d'Art de Catalunya (MNAC). An outdoor museum called Poble Espanyol recreates a typical Spanish village so that visitors can get a sense of the rich architectural history of the nation. The Fundació Joan Miró pays tribute to the well-known artist by displaying his surrealistic works in a remarkable structure created by Josep Llus Sert.

A variety of chances exist in the park for sports enthusiasts to participate in their favorite pursuits. You can take guided tours that show you inside the famous Montjuc Olympic Stadium, which served as the location for the 1992 Summer Olympics. Along the well-kept routes in the park, you can engage in several sports like running, cycling, or rollerblading. Montjuc Park is a sanctuary for picnickers thanks to its large green spaces, offering the ideal place to unwind and take it easy while eating outside.

Additionally, throughout the year, Montjuc Park is the site of several festivals and cultural events. There is usually something spectacular happening on its grounds, from music concerts and dance performances to film screenings and theater productions. Open-air venues in the park, like the Greek Theatre and the Montjuc Castle, provide the perfect setting for outstanding performances against a breathtaking backdrop.

The history and heritage of Barcelona are closely entwined with Montjuc Park, which offers more than just cultural and recreational opportunities.

You can find hidden jewels like the peaceful Montjuc Cemetery, which is filled with exquisite sculptures and spectacular views, by exploring the city's nooks and corners. The Montjuc Communications Tower, a recognizable reminder of the city's role in the 1992 Summer Olympics, is another place you can go. Take an elevator up to the observation deck for a bird's-eye perspective.

Park de la Ciutadella

In Barcelona, Park de la Ciutadella is one of the most adored and active parks. It is a beloved destination for both locals and tourists since it is conveniently located in the center of the city and offers a variety of activities and attractions. There is no shortage of entertainment to be obtained Qinside the park's expansive grounds, which have a rich history, gorgeous scenery, and a variety of amenities.

You'll be enthralled by the park's breathtaking beauty the moment you arrive. Your surroundings are lush vegetation, offering a welcome respite from the busy city streets. The Cascada Monumental, a stunning cascade created by Josep Fontsére and constructed for the Universal Exhibition in 1888, is the focal point of the park. Your awe at its majesty and complexity will make it the ideal location for photos or just to sit and appreciate the craftsmanship.

The boating lake is where you should go if you're up for some excitement. To navigate the calm waters and take in the beautiful scenery, you can rent a rowboat or a pedal boat. It's a wonderful activity to enjoy with friends or family on a beautiful afternoon while making lifelong memories.

The Park de la Ciutadella offers a lot to individuals who value art and culture. The Barcelona Zoo, which contains a broad range of animal species and provides educational activities for all ages, is one of the museums located in the park. Another amazing museum where you may discover more about animal life is the Museu de Zoologia.

The park offers plenty of areas for sports and entertainment if you're in the mood to get moving. Join a round of football or volleyball in the open fields, or challenge your pals to a friendly game of basketball on one of the many courts. As you bike through the park's many routes and trails, you can also rent a bicycle to explore it while taking in the scenery and fresh air.

A trip to the Catalan Parliament at Park de la Ciutadella is a must for any trip to the park. With features of both Gothic and Neoclassical architecture, this majestic structure is a work of art. Learn about the Catalan Parliament's past and current role while enjoying its gorgeous interior and minute features by taking a guided tour.

When it's time to unwind, pick a comfortable position in one of the park's several picnic sites. Gather your loved ones for a leisurely supper in the serene setting with a delectable buffet of regional specialties and a bottle of wine in tow. As an alternative, you can stop by one of the attractive cafés or kiosks in the park and savor some authentic Spanish foods like paella or churros.

The park has a ton of entertainment alternatives for families with kids. Playgrounds with swings, slides, and climbing frames let kids burn off some energy. Little ones love puppet shows and storytelling sessions at their favorite place, The Puppet House. Moreover, if you go in the summer, don't forget to take advantage of the splash pools in the park, where water jets and fountains create a cool oasis.

The park acquires a lovely aura as the day gives way to night. Take in the atmosphere as you stroll down the lit paths while taking in the music and performances of the street artists. Always check the schedule for any scheduled performances because the park frequently holds live concerts and cultural events. Visitors of all ages will always find something to amuse and delight them, from classical music to traditional dancing.

Park del Laberint d'Horta

In Barcelona, Spain, there is a wonderful green haven called Park del Laberint d'Horta, which provides a wide range of enjoyable and amusing activities. This park is the ideal location for individuals seeking enjoyment, relaxation, and a hint of magic with its beautiful gardens, enchanted labyrinth, and peaceful atmosphere.

The Labyrinth, a maze that offers an exciting experience to guests of all ages, is the focal point of the park. You enter a realm of mystery and intrigue the moment you step inside the labyrinth. Curiosity and awe are sparked by the towering, immaculately maintained hedges. As you navigate the labyrinth's twists and turns in search of the elusive exit, the challenge of finding your way through it is both exciting and humorous. The labyrinth offers a fun and fascinating experience that will hold your attention for hours, whether you choose to explore the maze by yourself or compete with friends and family.

The park also has stunning gardens that are a feast for the senses outside of the labyrinth. Take a stroll down the twisting trails and let the flower's vivid colors and alluring scents sweep you away. For a relaxing picnic or a friendly game of frisbee, the immaculately kept grounds make the ideal environment. The peace of nature can be simply savored by finding a comfortable position in the shade of a tree or lying down on the grass.

Park del Laberint d'Horta offers a visual feast for those who enjoy both art and architecture. Elegant pavilions, elaborate fountains, and fine statues may all be found in the 18th-century-designed neoclassical park. You'll be in awe of the picturesque landscape that is the result of the harmonious fusion of natural and artificial components.

Various attractive trails in the park loop around its vast grounds if you feel like taking a stroll. You'll come across tucked-away nooks and crannies along these routes, each with its charm and surprises. To stop, think, and take in the beauty of your surroundings, look for hidden benches, enticing nooks, and vantage spots.

Children can let their imaginations run wild in Park del Laberint d'Horta. When playing out daring explorers on a search for treasure, kids may let their imaginations run wild as they explore the labyrinth. There are plenty of possibilities for children to run around, play, and burn off steam in the park's open areas and playgrounds. They can engage in a thrilling game of hide-and-seek, scale the colorful sculptures, or simply take in the beauty of being surrounded by nature.

To heighten the excitement of your visit, the park also conducts several events and activities throughout the year. There is usually something going on at Park del Laberint d'Horta, from music concerts and art exhibitions to cultural festivals and outdoor theater performances. These occasions offer an opportunity to interact with the local populace, savor the rich Catalan culture, and make priceless memories.

Find a quiet area in the park as the day draws to a close to see a magnificent sunset. The peaceful waters of the park's ponds are transformed into a stunning display by the golden hues of the setting sun. Enjoy the beauty all around you for a moment, take a deep breath, and stop.

Tibidabo Amusement Park

An extraordinary experience may be had at Tibidabo Amusement Park in Barcelona, Spain, which is situated on the highest point of Collserola Ridge. Here, visitors can enjoy rides, thrilling attractions, and stunning scenery. Tibidabo, a must-visit attraction for both locals and tourists, has a long history that dates back to 1901 and offers a special fusion of old-world charm with new-world excitement.

When you first enter the park, a world of wonder and adventure is thrust into your lap. The Giradabo, a famous Ferris wheel in the park that provides sweeping views of the bustling city below, looms towering against the sky. Your breath will be taken away by the sheer height and stunningness of the surroundings, which creates the perfect atmosphere for an amazing day of enjoyment.

The Abismo roller coaster, which is one of Tibidabo's biggest draws, is exhilarating and certain to make your heart race. It's impossible to resist feeling the thrill of the ride as you soar through the air and maneuver at tremendous speeds. A heart-pounding sensation that will leave you wanting more is what The Abismo creates by fusing traditional roller coaster features with contemporary technology.

Tibidabo has many family-friendly attractions available for those looking for a more leisurely journey. Take in the stunning views of the city and the nearby Mediterranean Sea from the top of the Talaia, a serene observation tower that gently ascends. A traditional wooden roller coaster called the Muntanya Russa offers a nostalgic ride that is full of turns and twists and a touch of nostalgia. Each visitor can discover their brand of pleasure thanks to these attractions, which welcome people of all ages.

The theme park's rich history can be fully experienced at Tibidabo, which is more than just a location to go on rides. The museum inside the amusement park displays the development of theme parks and their relevance to popular culture. You can gain a look into the past and understand Tibidabo's origins by viewing old posters and ride artifacts.

You'll come across street performers, musicians, and artists as you stroll through the park, which will make your visit much more entertaining. Every part of Tibidabo is an experience in and of itself due to the dynamic environment and vibrant energy that creates a carnival-like vibe. You never know what surprises are around the corner, whether it's a fascinating street performance or a skilled artist working on a masterpiece right in front of you.

The dedication of Tibidabo to upholding tradition while welcoming innovation is one of its attractions. A variety of activities for guests of all ages are offered by the park's seamless integration of traditional attractions with cutting-edge rides. It is both charming and intriguing how this particular blending of the old and contemporary generates a timeless quality.

The park's attraction is further enhanced by the numerous activities Tibidabo holds throughout the year. At Tibidabo, there is always something going on, from music festivals to fireworks displays. Your visit will be even more magical thanks to these opportunities to see the park from a fresh perspective.

The food must be mentioned in any discussion of Tibidabo, at the very least. From authentic Spanish tapas to global fare, the park provides a wide variety of delectable gastronomic treats. Every palate can be satisfied, whether they are in the mood for a delectable churro or a cool scoop of ice cream. A very memorable experience that adds to Tibidabo's overall appeal is dining deliciously while admiring the spectacular vistas of Barcelona.

Chapter 7

Barcelona's Food and Drink

Catalan Cuisine

Catalan cuisine is renowned for its intense flavors, top-quality ingredients, and inventive flavor combinations. Traditional Catalan cuisine can be enjoyed in Barcelona, the capital of Catalonia, which has a thriving food scene. In Barcelona, you should taste these five Catalan dishes:

1. Paella: Originally from Valencia, paella has gained popularity across Catalonia and is a traditional Spanish meal. This meal, which is made with rice, is outstanding in Barcelona. Paella is a dish comprised of saffron-infused rice, chicken, rabbit, vegetables, and seafood that is often prepared in a sizable flat pan. Seafood paella, mixed paella, and Valencian paella are just a few of the many varieties of paella available. Famous in Barcelona for its mouthwatering paellas, El Raco de l'Agüir is a restaurant worth visiting.

2. Escudella I Carn d'Olla: This substantial stew from Catalonia is excellent during the winter. Various vegetables, including potatoes, cabbage, turnips, and carrots, are blended with a meat broth, typically produced from beef, hog, and chicken, in this classic dish. With rice or pasta, it is frequently served. A great escudella I carn d'olla is available in Can Culleretes, one of Barcelona's oldest eateries.

3. Crema Catalana: This delectable delicacy from Catalonia is a creamy custard-like concoction. It is prepared by heating milk, egg yolks, sugar, and lemon zest together, letting them cool, and then setting them in the refrigerator. A crisp sugar crust is created by caramelizing the top layer just before serving. The dessert is a Barcelona must-try. Restaurant Martnez serves up a delicious crema catalana.

4. Fideuà: Fideuà is a mouthwatering dish that resembles paella but utilizes fideos, which are thin, short noodles, in place of rice. Fish, shellfish, squid, and a savory broth are used to prepare this seafood-based cuisine, which has its roots in Catalonia's coastal regions. It is prepared similarly to paella. It's common to enjoy a great fideuà at Can Majó, a restaurant in Barcelona that's close to the beach.

5. Calcots with Romesco Sauce: Calcots, a kind of green onion unique to Catalonia, are a popular food in the region. Usually cooked till blackened and served with romesco sauce, these long, thin onions are long and thin. A tasty sauce known as Romesco is created by roasting red peppers, tomatoes, almonds, garlic, olive oil, and vinegar. It's a Catalan gastronomic experience you shouldn't pass up to eat charred calcots coated in zesty romesco sauce. There are delectable calcots and romesco sauce to be had at Can Travi Nou, a well-known restaurant in Barcelona.

With these five Catalan dishes, you may get a taste of Barcelona's diverse culinary history. Barcelona provides a variety of culinary experiences that will satisfy your cravings for food while also leaving you wanting more. These experiences range from the well-known paella to the comfortable escudella I carn d'olla and the sweet delight of crema catalana. To fully experience the rich Catalan cuisine culture, be sure to visit the city's food markets, tapas bars, and authentic restaurants. Grazie mille!

Best Restaurants and Cafes

Barcelona has a wide variety of outstanding restaurants and cafes that are sure to tempt your taste buds, whether you're looking for a cozy café or an elegant dining experience. The following list includes some of the city's top eateries:

1. El Celler de Can Roca: El Celler de Can Roca is one of the world's top restaurants and is a gastronomic treasure. Ingenious cooking methods are combined with traditional Catalan ingredients by the three Roca brothers to produce remarkable dishes. This three-Michelin-star restaurant ensures an exceptional dining experience with superb service and an exquisite wine list.

2. Disfrutar: Disfrutar is a molecular gastronomy restaurant in Barcelona run by former El Bulli chefs. Ingenious culinary displays and vibrant flavors are on display at the restaurant, which takes a contemporary and artistic approach to cooking. Disfrutar, a restaurant with two Michelin stars, is a haven for foodies looking for an uncommon and avant-garde dining experience.

3. Tickets: Designed by renowned chef Albert Adrià and located in the center of Barcelona,

Tickets is a cutting-edge tapas bar. Innovative tapas and imaginative cocktails are served at this Michelin-starred restaurant, providing a quirky dining experience. Tickets are a must-visit due to the jovial ambiance and outstanding gastronomic treats.

4. Dos Palillos: Located in the lively El Raval area, Dos Palillos combines Asian and Mediterranean tastes to produce a delicious fusion meal. Innovative recipes are created by chef Albert Raurich, a former student of Ferran Adrià. Modern furnishings and an open kitchen enhance the dining experience overall.

5. Can Majó: Visit Can Majó for some real fish from Catalonia. For more than 50 years, this family-run restaurant has been serving delectable seafood dishes in the charming Barceloneta district. Each taste celebrates the aromas of the Mediterranean, from paella to grilled fish.

6. Cervecera Catalana: Both locals and visitors like visiting this lively tapas pub. Cervecera Catalana provides a genuine sense of Barcelona with its extensive tapas menu and lively environment. Don't miss their patatas bravas, which are fried potatoes that are crunchy and served with a hot tomato sauce.

7. Brunch & Cake: This establishment is the best choice if you're in the mood for a delectable brunch. This café, well-known for its Instagram-worthy food and imaginative menu, provides a variety of brunch options, from pancakes to eggs Benedict. It is a well-known location for breakfast or brunch due to the welcoming ambiance and helpful staff.

8. Satan's Coffee Corner: This is a coffee lover's must-visit location. This specialized coffee business, which is situated in the hip El Raval district, is renowned for its expertly brewed beverages and relaxed ambiance. Take a sip of their famous flat white or get some advice from the welcoming baristas.

9. Granja M. Viader: Travel back in time to Granja M. Viader, a historic café that has been offering traditional Catalan sweets and dairy items since 1870. The velvety hot chocolate and "Cacaolat," a Catalan chocolate milkshake, are this delightful establishment's most well-known offerings. Take in the nostalgic atmosphere while enjoying a slice of their handcrafted pastries.

Traditional Dishes and Tapas

1. Paella: A mainstay of Barcelona's culinary scene, paella is a traditional Spanish rice dish. Paella is a vibrant dish that captures the spirit of Mediterranean cooking. It is made with saffron-infused rice, a range of meats (including chicken, rabbit, and shellfish), and vegetables.

2. Crema Catalana: This delicacy, which is a creamy custard with a caramelized sugar topping, is regarded as the Catalan equivalent of crème brûlée. If you have a sweet tooth, you must try this delicious dessert that is flavored with lemon zest and cinnamon.

3. Escalivada: A classic combination of grilled veggies in this Catalan cuisine are red peppers, eggplant, and onions. Olive oil, salt, and pepper are added to the roasted vegetables after they have been cooked till tender. As a side dish or a topping for bread, escalivada is frequently offered.

4. Fideuà: Is a seafood meal that, like paella, uses thin noodles in place of rice. A savory broth is used to cook noodles with a variety of shellfish, including mussels, shrimp, and squid. For those who want to try something new yet equally wonderful, Fideuà is a delightful substitute.

5. Patatas Bravas: This popular tapa from Barcelona consists of crispy fried potatoes that are accompanied by a hot tomato sauce and garlic aioli. In practically every tapas bar in the city, you can get this well-liked meal, which is great for sharing with friends.

6. Gambas al Ajillo: The availability of fresh fish alternatives in Barcelona is a result of its proximity to the Mediterranean Sea. A traditional tapa is called gambas al ajillo, and it consists of prawns cooked in olive oil flavored with garlic and a touch of chili. Frequently paired with a glass of regional wine, this dish is straightforward but tasty.

7. Pan with Tomate: This Catalan classic is a straightforward yet delectable preparation of toasted bread that has been rubbed with juicy tomatoes and topped with olive oil. It frequently functions as a basis for different toppings or as a side dish to other cuisines.

8. Calcots with Romesco Sauce: Calcots, a kind of delicious spring onion, are a Catalan region delicacy. They are typically grilled over an open flame until charred and then served with romesco sauce, an aromatic concoction of roasted red peppers, garlic, almonds, and olive oil. The calçotada season, a traditional Catalan holiday, is when this meal is most popular.

9. Pimientos de Padrón: Pimientos de Padrón are little green peppers that have been fried till blistered and then salted. Although most of the peppers in this tapa are moderate, now and then you'll come across a fiery one, giving each mouthful a pleasant surprise.

10. Canelons: Despite their origins in Italy, canelons have grown to be a beloved staple of Catalan cuisine. Canelons, which are traditionally consumed on Boxing Day or New Year's Eve, are packed with leftover meats such as roasted lamb or beef, combined with béchamel sauce, and grated with cheese. This filling dish is an adaptation of an Italian classic with Catalan flavors.

You will discover numerous additional scrumptious treats by exploring this bustling city's food scene. Barcelona is a gastronomic destination that guarantees to delight even the most discriminating palates, from the bustling food markets to the quaint local cafés.

Local Markets and Food Halls

Catalonia's dynamic capital city of Barcelona is well renowned for its diverse food scene. Numerous local markets and food halls can be found throughout the city, where they provide a wonderful selection of fresh foods, regional specialties, and flavors from around the world. These markets and food halls are must-visit locations, regardless of whether you're a food fanatic or are just interested in learning more about the city's culinary offerings.

1. La Boqueria: The most well-known market in Barcelona is La Boqueria, which is situated on the famed La Rambla Street. With a history dating back to the 13th century, it provides a wide range of fruits, vegetables, seafood, meats, cheeses, and spices. Along with various pubs and stalls, the market offers a variety of restaurants where you can eat tapas, fresh juices, and traditional Catalan fare.

2. Mercat de Sant Josep de la Boqueria: Known as Mercat de Sant Josep, this bustling market is located in the Eixample neighborhood. In addition to fruits, vegetables, meats, and seafood, it displays a large range of fresh produce. The market is a favorite hangout for both locals and visitors because of its lively exhibits and lively atmosphere.

3. Mercat de Santa Caterina: This up-to-date market has a vibrant, undulating ceiling and is situated in the hip El Born district. Fresh fruits, vegetables, meats, seafood, and regional delicacies are all available in great variety at the market. It is also home to a variety of eateries where you can savor authentic Catalan fare.

4. Mercat de Sant Antoni: Mercat de Sant Antoni reopened in 2018 after undergoing substantial renovations and is now a well-liked hangout for foodies. Along with numerous booths selling clothing, accessories, and antiques, the market offers a wide variety of fresh fruit. A Sunday market is held there as well, where you can discover uncommon products like vinyl records and books.

5. Mercat de la Concepció: Located in the Eixample neighborhood, Mercat de la Concepció is a lovely market popular for its flower shops and fresh goods. Gourmet goods, spices, and specialty foods are available at the market in addition to a huge selection of fruits, vegetables, and flowers. A fast snack can be had at one of the market's cafés or materials can be purchased for a picnic there.

6. Mercat del Ninot: Is a modern market that just received a thorough refurbishment, is located in the Eixample neighborhood of Barcelona. The market has a contemporary aesthetic and provides a wide selection of goods, such as fresh fruits, vegetables, meats, and cheeses. There are also several taverns and eateries there where you can enjoy delectable tapas and regional cuisine.

7. Els Encants Vells: Known as Barcelona's oldest flea market, Els Encants Vells is a haven for bargain hunters and collectors of vintage items. In addition to antiques, apparel, electronics, and home goods, the market offers a wide variety of products. You can experience regional specialties and street food in the food section as well.

8. Palo Alto Market: A buzzing event that blends cuisine, art, and design, Palo Alto Market takes place on specified Sundays. A hand-picked assortment of independent designers, artists, and gourmet food vendors are featured. Additionally, the market hosts workshops, live music performances, and other events that add to the lively and joyful ambiance.

9. Espai Gastronmic Mercat Princesa: Located in the El Born area, Mercat Princesa is a distinctive food hall built inside a former palace. Catalan, Spanish, Asian, and Latin American cuisines are just a few of the many cuisines available at the space's many food vendors. In a buzzing, friendly environment, it's a great spot to eat a variety of meals.

10. El Mercat de Sant Antoni: This market, which is located in Barcelona's Sant Antoni area, is one of the city's oldest and most well-established. Fresh fruits, vegetables, meats, fish, and other delectables are available in plenty there. While the indoor market is being renovated, the outside market is still open and still selling a variety of fruits, vegetables, and flowers.

Wine and Cava Tasting

An elegant celebration of the rich history and expert workmanship of Catalan wines and cavas is the Wine and Cava Tasting of Barcelona. Barcelona, a bustling city renowned for its artistic riches, architectural marvels, and culinary delights, is the setting for this yearly event. Wine lovers, experts, and tourists with an interest in wine from around the world assemble to partake in a sensory tour of the best vintages produced in the area.

The event takes place in a scenic setting, frequently in a charming courtyard or a historic building that oozes Barcelona's special charm. Elegant accents, subdued lighting, and melodic live music in the background create an elegant atmosphere. A welcoming and laid-back atmosphere is what Wine and Cava Tasting strives to achieve so that visitors can enjoy the flavors and fragrances of Catalonia's well-known libations.

When visitors arrive, welcoming hosts hand them a sample glass, a program booklet, and a map highlighting the various wineries and cavas taking part in the event. The pamphlet acts as a guide, providing comprehensive details about each wine company, including their history, winemaking processes, and the qualities of their wines.

Wines are tasted first throughout the tasting process. Catalonia offers a wide variety of terroirs and grape varietals, which produce a wide range of reds, whites, and rosés. Every taste may find something to savor, from the strong and substantial red wines of Priorat to the crisp and energizing whites of Penedès. Sommeliers with years of experience are available to share their knowledge and guide customers in understanding the subtleties of each vintage by providing insights into the wines.

As the tasting goes on, the cava, Catalonia's well-known sparkling wine, assumes center stage. The traditional technique of production results in exquisite bubbles and rich tastes in cavas since they are made with great care and go through a second fermentation in the bottle. The cava collection demonstrates the area's expertise in producing superb sparkling wines, from well-known houses to smaller boutique producers.

There are specially chosen meal pairings to go with the wines and cavas. Local specialties like artisanal cheeses, cured meats, fresh shellfish, and delicious tapas are perfectly paired with the drinks to improve the taste experience. The tastes blend to create pleasing combinations that tease the palate and show off the complex interactions between food and wine.

To gain a greater understanding of the artistry and passion that goes into each bottle, attendees have the chance to interact directly with winemakers and cava producers during the event. Through these contacts, visitors can gain first-hand knowledge of the vineyards, the wine-making process, and the distinctive tales behind each wine, further enhancing their experience.

The Wine and Cava Tasting of Barcelona also includes educational seminars and workshops run by professionals in the field in addition to the tastings. These lectures cover a variety of subjects, including wine pairing, the technique of sabrage (the act of cracking a bottle of cava with a saber), and the development of winemaking in Catalonia. Attendees leave these educational activities with a comprehensive knowledge of the viticulture of the area and its significance to the wine industry.

The chance to buy their preferred wines and cavas straight from the producers is offered to attendees as the event comes to a close. The close relationship between wine lovers and vintners is strengthened by this interaction, which also contributes to the wine industry's sustainability in Catalonia.

The Barcelona Wine and Cava Tasting is a celebration of Catalan heritage, culture, and the delight of exchanging amazing experiences, not simply of wine and cava. It embodies the atmosphere of Barcelona's vivacious city and enables visitors to go on a delightful exploration of the area's extraordinary vinicultural legacy. This event guarantees an incredible adventure that will make a lasting imprint on your senses and your heart, whether you are an experienced oenophile or simply keen to learn more about the world of wine.

Chapter 8

Shopping in Barcelona

Popular Shopping Streets

1. La RamblaLa Rambla: Is unquestionably the most well-known and recognizable boulevard in Barcelona. From Plaça de Catalunya to the Christopher Columbus Monument in Port Vell, it is a busy pedestrian avenue that is lined with stores, cafes, restaurants, and street performers for 1.2 kilometers. From trinkets and regional crafts to clothing stores and bookshops, you can find anything here.

2. Passeig de Gràcia: This premium neighborhood's prime upscale shopping boulevard is called Passeig de Gràcia and is situated in

Barcelona. It is a sanctuary for those who love fashion, lined with high-end labels like Gucci, Chanel, and Louis Vuitton. In addition, the street is well known for its masterpiece buildings, such as Casa Batlló and Casa Milà, both of which were created by renowned architect Antoni Gaud.

3. Portal de l'ngel: Located in the center of Barcelona's Gothic Quarter, Portal de l"ngel is a lively shopping avenue renowned for its large selection of retail establishments. This pedestrian boulevard offers a varied shopping experience, with multinational companies like H&M and Sephora alongside well-known Spanish retailers like Zara and Mango. Visiting nearby jewelry and accessories stores is also a fantastic idea.

4. Diagonal Avenue: Cutting diagonally through the city, Diagonal Avenue is a main artery in Barcelona. The busy traffic on this street is not the only thing that makes it popular; there are also lots of places to shop. El Corte Inglés department stores and shopping centers like L'Illa Diagonal, which has a range of businesses, eateries, and a movie theater, can be found nearby.

5. Carrer de Sants: The 4.2-kilometer-long Carrer de Sants, which is found in Barcelona's Sants-Montjuc neighborhood, is the city's longest shopping strip. Local boutiques, well-known fashion chains, and neighborhood stores are all represented on this bustling boulevard. It is a favorite with residents and tourists seeking an experience that is more authentically local and away from the tourist hordes.

6. El Born: Situated in the quaint El Born neighborhood, this area is renowned for its winding lanes dotted with chic boutiques and clothing stores. Fashion-conscious people looking for distinctive apparel, accessories, and independent designers will love El Born. The well-known Mercat del Born, a cultural hub that holds performances and exhibitions, is also located in the neighborhood.

7. Gràcia: Gràcia is Barcelona's bohemian district and a hidden gem for shopping. Unique, independent stores selling handcrafted goods, vintage apparel, and one-of-a-kind souvenirs line the small streets of this town. In addition to its bustling squares and charming cafes, Gràcia is renowned for its lively environment, which allows visitors to relax after a long day of shopping and take in the culture.

8. Avinguda de Gaud: This pedestrian boulevard, which is named for the visionary architect Antoni Gaud, is situated in the Eixample neighborhood. A variety of stores, cafes, and eateries are available on this street, with a focus on Catalan and Mediterranean fare. Gourmet food, fine wines, and regional specialties can all be found there in abundance.

9. Carrer de Verdi: Located in the hip Gràcia district of Barcelona, Carrer de Verdi is a bustling street dotted with distinctive stores, galleries, and independent boutiques. It is well known for its bohemian vibe and is a terrific destination to find handcrafted jewelry, vintage apparel, and original artwork. Verdi Park, a pleasant green park ideal for a stroll, is located on the same street.

10. Rambla de Catalunya: Running parallel to Passeig de Gràcia, Rambla de Catalunya is a broad, upscale promenade that provides a more laid-back shopping experience. There are a variety of specialty stores, boutiques, and charming cafes with outdoor terraces in this area. A cup of coffee, leisurely shopping, or simply soaking up the ambiance of the city are all great things to do there.

Unique Local Boutiques

1. Santa Eulalia: Located in the center of Barcelona, Santa Eulalia is a prominent shop noted for its upscale clothing and accessories. Gucci, Balenciaga, and Saint Laurent are among the high-end labels that they provide.

2. Vinçon: Located in the Eixample neighborhood, Vinçon is a design concept store with a distinctive collection of cookware, home furnishings, and other lifestyle goods.

3. The Apartment: The Apartment is an interior design, fashion, and art-focused store that is located in the Gothic Quarter. It is a must-visit for anyone who loves the arts because it exhibits up-and-coming designers and showcases their work.

4. Rita Row: A boutique for eco-friendly clothing in the Gràcia district, specializes in fair-trade garments made of natural materials. For both men and women, Rita Row has fashionable, sustainable clothes.

5. La Comercial: This store, which has sites all around the city, carries a carefully picked assortment of luxury clothing, accessories, and home goods. Each shop offers distinctive goods and a distinct environment.

6. La Manual Alpargatera: La Manual Alpargatera has been making espadrilles since 1940 and is well known for its classic styles. In their store in the El Raval district, you can find a broad selection of espadrilles for men, women, and kids.

7. Le Fortune: Located in the Born district, Le Fortune is a vintage store that carries a carefully curated selection of used apparel, accessories, and retro goods. Unique and one-of-a-kind items can be found there in abundance.

8. Custo Barcelona: Custo Barcelona is a well-known fashion label that was established in Barcelona and is distinguished by its vivid and colorful designs. The newest collections are on display at their store in the Born neighborhood.

9. La Boqueria Market: Although it is not a conventional store, La Boqueria Market is a must-see location for foodies. This famous market, which can be found outside Las Ramblas, sells a broad range of fresh fruits, vegetables, meats, and other regional specialties.

10. Le Swing Vintage: Is a mecca for lovers of vintage clothing and is located in the Raval district of Barcelona. Vintage apparel, accessories, and even vinyl recordings can all be found in a variety of styles.

11. Olokuti: This one-of-a-kind store, which is located in the Gràcia district, advocates for fair trade, sustainable development, and environmentally friendly goods. Their selection of clothing, accessories, household goods, and natural cosmetics is extensive.

12. Mshü: This Gothic Quarter store is home to Mshü, which specializes in traditional Japanese attire and accessories. They display stunning yukatas, kimonos, and other clothing with Japanese influences.

13. Holala! Plaza: Located in the Raval district, this vintage shop has a large selection of retro and vintage goods from many decades, including apparel, accessories, and furniture. A vintage enthusiast's dream comes true.

14. Fashion shop Lurdes Bergada: Is located in the El Born district and is well-known for its avant-garde and minimalist creations. Both men and women can purchase fashionable, modern apparel from them.

15. Estiarte: If you're an avid sports fan, Estiarte is a store that specializes in designer sports apparel and accessories. Cycling, running, swimming, and outdoor activities are their focus, and they feature quality goods.

Shopping Malls

1. La Roca Village: La Roca Village is a premier outlet shopping destination, located not far from Barcelona. There are more than 100 boutiques there with deals on designer goods from well-known fashion and lifestyle brands.

2. Maremagnum: This well-known shopping area, located in Port Vell, mixes retail therapy with breathtaking views of the ocean. It is home to a variety of shops, including those selling clothing, accessories, cosmetics, technology, and a wide selection of eateries.

3. Diagonal Mar: This up-to-date mall, which is situated close to the shore, offers a broad selection of international brands, shops, and entertainment alternatives. A sizable hypermarket, a multiplex theater, and an outdoor patio are further features of Diagonal Mar.

4. L'illa Diagonal: Located in the busy Avinguda Diagonal, L'illa Diagonal is a seasoned mall that provides a selection of upscale clothing, accessories, and home goods. It also has a sizable supermarket and several dining establishments.

5. Glries: A vibrant shopping complex that just underwent a facelift, Glries is situated next to the famous Torre Agbar. It features a wide variety of retail establishments, including clothing, electronics, and home furnishings, as well as a movie theater and a variety of dining alternatives.

6. Gran Via 2: This sizable mall, which is close to the Fira de Barcelona convention center, specializes in selling fashion, accessories, and lifestyle goods. It has a food court, a movie theater, and many international brands.

7. Arenas de Barcelona: Located in a former bullring, Arenas de Barcelona is a distinctive place to shop. It has a varied assortment of shops, eateries, and a rooftop terrace offering expansive city views.

8. El Triangle: This compact yet energetic shopping district is located right in the middle of Barcelona's Gothic Quarter. It has a variety of shops, including ones for fashion, cosmetics, and technology, in addition to a sizable FNAC bookshop.

9. La Maquinista: One of Barcelona's biggest shopping centers, La Maquinista offers a wide variety of shops, activities, and restaurants. It has an open-air design that makes shopping there enjoyable.

10. Splau: This contemporary shopping center, which is situated outside of Barcelona, offers a wide variety of goods and services. It has a large variety of shops, a multi-screen theater, and a sizable food court.

11. Heron City Barcelona: Located close to the Forum district, Heron City Barcelona is a distinctive entertainment complex that mixes dining, shopping, and recreational pursuits. It has a combination of shops, a multiplex theater, lanes for bowling, and a range of dining options.

12. La Maquinista Sant Andreu: This retail center is situated in the Sant Andreu neighborhood and offers a variety of national and international brands. A movie theater and a variety of restaurants are also located there.

13. Les Glries Shopping Centre: This shopping center, which is next to the Agbar Tower, recently completed renovations that transformed it into a sleek and contemporary shopping destination. It has a variety of shops, dining options, and a rooftop deck.

14. El Corte Inglés: Although not a mall per se, El Corte Inglés needs to be mentioned due to its importance as the largest department store chain in Spain. It has a large assortment of products in many departments at its flagship shop in Barcelona, which is situated on Plaça de Catalunya.

Chapter 9

Day Trips from Barcelona

Montserrat

Near Barcelona, Spain is the breathtaking mountain range known as Montserrat. It's a well-liked day trip location for visitors to Barcelona due to its majesty peaks, stunning vistas, and the renowned Montserrat Abbey. Montserrat has a wide range of things to do and places to see because of its fascinating history, stunning scenery, and cultural significance.

As you set off on your day vacation, the ride from Barcelona to Montserrat is a thrilling experience in and of itself. There are numerous transit alternatives accessible, and the mountain range is situated around 50 kilometers northwest of

Barcelona. The most practical means of transportation to go to Montserrat is by train. Trains frequently leave from Plaça d'Espanya in Barcelona, taking passengers on a beautiful excursion through the Catalan countryside. As you travel by train, you may take in the beautiful scenery and get in shape for the delights Montserrat has to offer.

The majestic vista of the serrated mountain peaks that give the area its name will greet you as you arrive in Montserrat. Against the brilliant blue skies, the unusual rock formations and rocky cliffs make a striking backdrop. The Montserrat Abbey, a Benedictine monastery perched high on the mountainside, ought to be one of your first destinations on your day trip. The abbey is well known for its spectacular architecture, as well as its importance to religion and culture. You can tour the Basilica inside the monastery, which houses the well-known statue of the Black Madonna, commonly known as La Moreneta. People come to this revered statue to pay their respects and ask for blessings from it from all over the world.

After exploring the abbey, spend some time exploring the many hiking routes that wind through the highlands. You can select a route that meets your preferences and degree of fitness thanks to the variety of difficulties offered by these paths. Awe-inspiring perspectives that provide expansive views of the surrounding landscapes can be found as you go through the mountains. There are numerous options for photography aficionados to capture the beauty of Montserrat thanks to the combination of towering hills, verdant valleys, and far-off horizons.

Consider riding the cable car or funicular railway to the higher altitudes of Montserrat if you're looking for a little additional adventure. These modes of transportation offer an exciting ascent that enables you to reach elevated perspectives and discover remote areas of the mountain range. You can set out on more difficult climbs from the higher stations, find isolated chapels hidden in the mountainside, or just take in the tranquility of nature.

Not only is Montserrat a paradise for nature lovers, but it is also a center of culture. The mountain range plays host to several festivals and events all year long that highlight the local cuisine, dance, and music. If one of these events falls during your day excursion, you'll have the chance to experience the lively local culture firsthand and see how the Catalan way of life is practiced. These occasions bring an added level of excitement to your trip to Montserrat, from exhilarating musical performances to vibrant processions.

Don't pass up the chance to visit the Montserrat Museum to truly understand the cultural legacy of the island. This museum, located inside the abbey, is home to a substantial collection of artwork from many historical and stylistic periods. Masterworks by well-known artists including El Greco, Caravaggio, and Picasso, among others, can be seen here. Both art lovers and history aficionados should visit the museum since it provides a fascinating look into the historical and aesthetic legacy of Montserrat.

Take some time as your day excursion comes to an end to enjoy Montserrat's peace and think back on the experiences you've made. Montserrat is a special place because of its breathtaking scenery, meditative atmosphere, and sense of connection to the past and natural world. The day trip from Barcelona to Montserrat is a tour that will leave a lasting impression, whether you've explored the hiking trails, marveled at the abbey's architecture, or dived into the local culture.

You'll return to Barcelona with not only the breathtaking photos you took with your camera but also a sense of awe and wonder that can only be felt firsthand. Each time I visit Montserrat, I learn something new about its rich natural beauty, spirituality, and cultural significance. So, if you're in Barcelona and looking for an educational day excursion, go beyond the city and explore the breathtaking attraction of Montserrat.

Sitges

A day excursion from the busy city is excellent to the picturesque coastal village of Sitges, which is only 35 kilometers southwest of Barcelona. Sitges offer a wide range of sights and activities for tourists to enjoy thanks to its stunning beaches, lively culture, and rich history. We will examine some of the best day trips from Barcelona to Sitges in this post, emphasizing the major attractions and activities that make this town a must-see location.

Sitges' gorgeous coastline, which is lined with picturesque beaches, is one of the city's primary attractions. Playa de la Ribera, which is a short distance from the town center, is the most well-known and conveniently placed beach. The area offers guests a chance to unwind on the golden sands, enjoy the Mediterranean sun, and cool down in the pristine waters. The beach is well-equipped with services, such as beach bars, restaurants, and areas for participating in water sports, guaranteeing a pleasant and relaxing day by the sea.

Sitges is home to numerous architectural marvels and museums for anyone with an interest in history and culture. The Church of Sant Bartomeu I Santa Tecla, an opulent 17th-century church situated in the center of Sitges, is one of the town's most recognizable attractions. It is an attraction that is a must-see because of its striking exterior and elaborate interior decorations. Visitors can get a glimpse of the town's cultural legacy at the Cau Ferrat Museum and the Maricel Museum, which are close by and display a variety of works of art and artifacts by well-known artists including Santiago Rusiol and Ramon Casas.

The colorful festivals and events in Sitges are also well-known. The Sitges Carnival, a vibrant and exuberant celebration that takes place in February, is one of the most well-liked events. The streets come to life at this time with parades, fancy dress, music, and dancing, creating a joyful atmosphere that should not be missed. In addition, the Sitges Film Festival, which takes place in October, draws moviegoers from all over the world and features a large selection of premieres of foreign films.

There is a lot for nature enthusiasts to discover in Sitges as well. Visitors can find the stunning natural reserve known for its rocky landscapes, abundant greenery, and varied fauna not far from the town center, the Garraf Natural Park. The park's hiking trails give breathtaking views of the mountains and beach nearby. The Garraf Astronomical Observatory, located in the park, is a great place for astronomy buffs to view the glories of the night sky.

Without sampling the local cuisine, no trip to Sitges would be complete. Fresh fish and traditional Catalan cuisine are well-known in this town. Catalan-style tapas and sweet pastries are served alongside grilled sardines and paella in neighborhood restaurants and tapas bars. Every tourist to Sitges will have a wonderful dining experience thanks to the town's diverse dining options, which are suitable for all tastes and price ranges.

It is simple and convenient to travel from Barcelona to Sitges. Regular trains depart from Estació de Sants, the main train station in Barcelona, and go to Sitges in about 30 minutes. Buses are another option for traveling between the two cities; they offer a convenient and beautiful route along the shore.

Costa Brava

Catalonia's vivacious capital city of Barcelona is renowned for its dynamic atmosphere, gorgeous architecture, and rich history as well as for being close to the stunning Costa Brava. The Costa Brava region, which is on Spain's northeastern coast, is home to a stunning coastline, charming villages, and a wide range of recreational opportunities.

Cadaqués, a lovely village on the Costa Brava, is one of the most well-liked tourist destinations. Cadaqués has long drawn writers and painters because of its picturesque port, white-washed homes, and winding lanes. Enjoy some fresh seafood at a neighborhood eatery, take a stroll through the village, and stop by the Santa Maria Church. Don't forget to visit the Salvador Dali House Museum in Port Lligat, where the illustrious artist lived and created.

Visit the Cap de Creus Natural Park for a dose of the great outdoors. The craggy cliffs, secret coves, and pristine waters of this wild coastal park make it a haven for wildlife enthusiasts. Enjoy a trek through the trails, a picnic with stunning views, or just some downtime on a remote beach. You will be in awe of the magnificent views provided by the Cap de Creus Lighthouse, which is positioned atop a cliff.

Make your way next to Tossa de Mar, a historic settlement. With its winding cobblestone alleys, lovely homes, and imposing castle with a view of the sea, this picturesque town, which is surrounded by old walls, transports you back in time. Visit the stronghold in Vila Vella, wander through the winding streets, and unwind on the beautiful beaches. In addition, Tossa de Mar is home to many top-notch seafood eateries where you may sample the local cuisine.

Go to Lloret de Mar if you want to be in a more energetic environment. Even while Lloret de Mar is known for its vibrant nightlife, it also has stunning beaches and intriguing cultural activities. Visit the Santa Clotilde Gardens, a beautiful garden set on a cliff with breathtaking views of the Mediterranean. Discover the marine history of the town by visiting the Marine Museum, which is situated in a former lighthouse from the 19th century. Of course, enjoy the beach's bustling atmosphere and the sunshine as well.

Visit Salvador Dal's birthplace, Figueres, to get a flavor of the artistic past. A must-see attraction is the Dali Theatre Museum, which exhibits the quirky artist's creations in an unconventional environment. Get lost in Dal's imaginative world by exploring the bizarre displays. After that, stroll around the streets of Figueres, take in the wonderful architecture, and savor some Catalan food at the nearby eateries.

Visit the Aiguamolls de l'Empordà Natural Park if you want to feel nature's allure. Birdwatchers will find this wetland reserve to be a haven as it is home to a wide variety of bird species. Explore the trails at your leisure, look for herons, flamingos, and other local birds, and take in the peace of this natural haven. For individuals interested in learning more about ecology, the park also provides educational programs and guided excursions.

Last but not least, take advantage of the chance to visit Blanes, a beautiful beach town. Blanes, which is well-known for its stunning floral gardens, offers a fascinating fusion of natural beauty and historic legacy. Explore the Marimurtra Botanical Garden to see a wide variety of exotic plants from all over the world. It is set on a rock overlooking the sea. Enjoy the sandy beaches, stroll along the Passeig de Dintre promenade, and take in this delightful town's laid-back vibe.

The day tours from Barcelona to the Costa Brava provide a unique experience through the splendor of Catalonia, from lively seaside villages to beautiful natural reserves. The Costa Brava has everything, whether you're looking for culture, nature, art, or just a quiet getaway. So get ready to go, experience these thrilling adventures, and make lifelong memories.

Girona

The picturesque city of Girona, which is close to Barcelona, is one such location that needs to be on every traveler's itinerary. With the help of this tour, you can virtually explore Girona's top attractions and learn about the best day trips you can do from Barcelona to fully enjoy your stay.

A hidden jewel with a plethora of historical and cultural riches, Girona is frequently eclipsed by its bigger neighbor. With its quaint cobblestone alleys, historic fortifications, and striking Gothic architecture, its well-preserved medieval old town is a treat to explore. Take the train to Girona from Barcelona to start your day excursion; it's a quick and easy way to get there. To make the most of your time in this wonderful city, the trip takes around an hour.

Make your way to the city's center, where the towering Girona Cathedral is located, as soon as you arrive in Girona. This famous structure dominates the skyline with its imposing bell tower and provides stunning city views from its rooftop. Before going inside to see the cathedral's elaborate interior, take a minute to ponder the complex intricacies of its exterior.

After that, explore the tangled alleys of the Barri Vell, the city's historic district, where you'll find lovely squares, endearing cafes, and specialty stores. Spend some time in the medieval ambiance as you stroll down the Onyar River, which is bordered by vibrant houses that make for a picture-perfect scene. To get across the river and find more undiscovered nooks of the city, cross the renowned Pont de les Peixateries Velles, a stunning iron bridge.

The Jewish Quarter, a historic district that goes back to the Middle Ages, is one of the must-see attractions in Girona. Discover its winding lanes and alleyways, and stop by the Museum of Jewish History, which offers a fascinating look into the city's vibrant Jewish history.

The Girona Art Museum should not be missed by art lovers. This museum, which is located in the Episcopal Palace, has a remarkable collection of Catalan artwork from many historical periods, such as the medieval, Renaissance, and contemporary movements. Learn more about the area's artistic past while admiring works of art by well-known painters.

If you enjoy watching Game of Thrones, you'll be happy to learn that Girona was used as a filming site. Take a self-guided tour to see the famous locations where sequences from the show were shot, like the Cathedral's stairwell, which was changed to seem like the Great Sept of Baelor. Immerse yourself in the land of Westeros by following in the footsteps of your favorite characters.

The native cuisine is a must-try during every trip to Girona. The city has a thriving culinary scene with a vast selection of delectable foods. Enjoy typical Catalan cuisine, like pa amb tomàquet (bread with tomato), fideuà (a noodle dish akin to paella), and crema catalana (a creamy custard dessert). For a truly unique dining experience, serve your meal with a glass of regional wine or cava, Catalonia's sparkling wine.

If you have extra time, think about leaving Girona's city boundaries to visit the surrounding countryside. Vineyards, historic villages, and gorgeous vistas are all features of the area. Take a quick bus ride to Besal, a quaint village famous for its intact medieval bridge and Jewish history. Alternatively, go to Cadaqués, a lovely coastal village that was Salvador Dali's go-to getaway.

Return to Barcelona with fond memories of your day trip to Girona as the day draws to a close. Girona is the ideal getaway from the crowded streets of Barcelona, whether you choose to immerse yourself in its ancient history, awe at its architectural marvels, or savor its culinary delicacies. So gather your belongings, board a train, and see the enchantment of Girona materialize before your very eyes.

Tarragona

Just a short distance from Barcelona, along the stunning Costa Dorada, is the old city of Tarragona. It is one of these enthralling locations. We'll delve into Tarragona's attractions in this 1,000-word guide, emphasizing the city's fascinating past, gorgeous architecture, breathtaking coastline, and active cultural scene.

A remarkable historical legacy draws tourists from all over the world to Tarragona, which was originally the Roman capital of Hispania Tarraconensis. The Tarragona Amphitheatre, a well-preserved Roman amphitheater that formerly staged exciting gladiator battles and other events, is the most recognizable structure in the city. It nearly sounds like the past is still echoing as you walk through the old ruin sites, taking you back to the opulence of the Roman Empire.

The Tarragona Circus, a historic chariot race circuit, is situated next to the amphitheater. Imagine the adrenaline-fueled races that once enthralled spectators as you stroll over the track's ruins, and let yourself be transported back to the atmosphere of ancient Roman entertainment. A fantastic location for obtaining priceless photos is at the nearby Roman Walls, which date back to the third century and offer a panoramic view of the city and the Mediterranean Sea.

Without touring the Archaeological Ensemble of Tárraco, a UNESCO World Heritage Site in Tarragona, a trip to the city would be incomplete. The Roman Forum, the ancient city's beating heart, is a part of this enormous complex. Observe the beautifully preserved remains of temples, basilicas, and other buildings to obtain an understanding of Roman residents' daily lives.

You will come across quaint squares, lovely lanes, and historic structures as you stroll through the winding streets of Tarragona's Old Town, also referred to as Part Alta. With its spectacular Tarragona Cathedral and its fusion of Romanesque and Gothic styles, the skyline is dominated. Enter to take in the gorgeous interior, then climb the bell tower for sweeping views of the city and the surrounding countryside.

A similar allure can be found in Tarragona's coastline charm. You may relax and enjoy the Mediterranean sun on one of the city's many lovely beaches. Golden sands and crystal-clear waters characterize Tarragona's largest beach, Playa del Miracle, making it a great place for swimming and relaxing. Cala Fonda, also known as Waikiki Beach, is located in a tiny cove surrounded by rocks and pine trees and is the place to go if you want a more private atmosphere.

In addition to its historical and coastal charm, Tarragona offers a thriving cultural scene. Several cultural events and exhibitions are held at the Mediterranean Balcony, a contemporary sculpture that overlooks the water. A drink in hand while soaking in the spectacular sunsets that cast the city in a warm, golden light is the ideal activity at the Balcó del Mediterrani, a terrace with panoramic views.

Visit the National Archaeological Museum in Tarragona to learn more about the city's rich cultural legacy. This facility is home to a magnificent collection of Roman relics that shed light on Tarragona's past. For those who enjoy contemporary art, the Modern Art Museum of Tarragona features a wide selection of pieces by national and international creators, providing a singular viewpoint on the present artistic landscape.

Also worth discovering are Tarragona's culinary treasures. Enjoy the famed seafood specialties of the area, which pay homage to the city's maritime history and include zarzuela de mariscos and suquet de peix, among others. For a genuinely authentic dining experience, sip on some of the bold reds from the Priorat or the crisp whites from the Penedès region.

Chapter 10

Nightlife and Entertainment

Bars and Clubs

1. Razzmatazz: Is one of Barcelona's most well-known clubs, with many rooms playing various musical genres. It is situated in the Poblenou neighborhood.

2. Opium Barcelona: Located close to Barceloneta Beach, this hip club is renowned for its beachfront patio and hopping nightlife.

3. Sutton Club: Sutton Club, located in the Uptown neighborhood of Barcelona, offers an opulent environment and draws a trendy audience with its high-end music and VIP rooms.

4. Shoko Barcelona: Featuring a blend of Asian and Mediterranean food, this beachside club in Port Olympic features a restaurant, lounge, and nightlife.

5. Eclipse Barcelona: Situated on the 26th level of the W Barcelona Hotel, Eclipse provides stunning city views in addition to an upscale atmosphere and an exceptional drink selection.

6. Catwalk Barcelona: This well-known club is located in the Gothic Quarter and offers several music-related events, such as house, techno, and hip-hop evenings.

7. Sala Apolo: This historic venue has been a staple of Barcelona's nightlife scene for many years and is well-known for its eclectic schedule of live music performances and DJ sets.

8. Pacha Barcelona: Pacha Barcelona, an extension of the well-known Ibiza club, offers a chic and glamorous setting with renowned DJs spinning electronic dance music.

9. Macarena Club: A small underground venue dedicated to electronic music, Macarena Club is tucked away in the El Raval district.

10. Bar Marsella: One of Barcelona's oldest bars and one of its most well-known, Bar Marsella was a favorite hangout for Picasso and Ernest Hemingway, among other artists and authors. It was founded in 1820. It focuses primarily on absinthe.

11. Dow Jones: Located in the Eixample neighborhood, this unusual bar offers an engaging stock market-like experience by letting drink prices change in response to supply and demand.

12. El Born Bar: Located in the hip El Born area, this bar has a laid-back, bohemian atmosphere that's great for drinking homemade drinks and meeting residents and visitors alike.

13. Bobby's Free: Popular for its retro-style design and laid-back ambiance, Bobby's Free is a bar that draws a wide variety of people and serves a variety of drinks and spirits.

14. Jamboree: Located in Plaça Reial, Jamboree is a storied jazz club that has been offering live performances of live music since 1960, exhibiting both local and international talent.

15. Magic Club Barcelona: Situated in the Gothic Quarter, Magic Club is a welcoming bar well-known for its magic-themed furnishings, welcoming staff, and inventive cocktails.

Flamenco Shows

Flamenco is a dynamic and alluring art form with roots in Spanish culture. It is a spectacle that stokes desire and arouses strong feelings. There are many possibilities to see this captivating dance form in Barcelona, the modern capital of Catalonia, which is well known for its vibrant cultural environment. This essay will go into the world of flamenco performances in Barcelona, examining the background, settings, acts, and the whole immersion experience.

Flamenco is a combination of several elements, including Romani, Moorish, and Jewish traditions, and it has its roots in the Andalusian region of southern Spain. With origins in the 18th century, this art form first flourished in the secluded spaces of cafes and taverns where artists would assemble to perform and exchange skills. Flamenco gradually found a place in Barcelona's cultural landscape as it grew in popularity and recognition through time and spread throughout Spain.

The hypnotic charm of flamenco is now showcased in a variety of locations throughout Barcelona. The Palau de la Msica Catalana, a UNESCO World Heritage Site known for its modernist architecture and outstanding acoustics, is one such location. This legendary concert venue regularly holds flamenco concerts, attracting both seasoned performers and up-and-coming musicians to mesmerize audiences with their rhythmic footwork, heartfelt singing, and complex guitar melodies.

The Tablao Cordobés, which is situated in the center of Barcelona's thriving Las Ramblas neighborhood, is another well-liked location for flamenco performances. With its cozy atmosphere, this table (a traditional flamenco venue) delivers an immersive experience, enabling viewers to directly experience the passion and intensity of flamenco. Reputable performers perform on stage and captivate viewers with their mesmerizing dance, moving vocals, and expressive gestures. The Tablao Cordobés also provides the opportunity to take advantage of a traditional Spanish meal choice, which enhances the overall experience.

The Tarantos Barcelona offers an alternative method of experiencing flamenco for those wanting a more unusual venue. This cozy theater, which is located in the picturesque Plaça Reial, provides nightly performances that feature both classic and avant-garde flamenco. Infusing their distinctive approaches into this work, the artists push the boundaries of the medium while remaining faithful to its core. The Tarantos Barcelona offers a stage for up-and-coming artists, making it a great option for those wanting to see flamenco advance.

In addition to these well-known locations, Barcelona is home to a large number of additional institutions that feature flamenco performances, from small, secluded settings to vast theaters.

Among these are Los Tarantos, Palau Dalmases, and El Tablao de Carmen. There is something for every aficionado thanks to how each location adds to the rich tapestry of flamenco experiences present throughout the city.

In Barcelona, going to a flamenco performance is more than just a passive activity; it's an immersion into the heart of Spanish culture. The atmosphere becomes electrified when the performers enter the stage, and the atmosphere grows more exciting. A magical ambiance is created that brings viewers to the essence of flamenco through the repetitive clapping, eerie melodies, and fascinating footwork.

Baile (dance), cante (song), and toque (guitar) are the three primary components of a traditional flamenco performance. With their exact footwork, beautiful arm motions, and expressive facial expressions, bailors (flamenco dancers) personify the passion and intensity of the art form. Flamenco guitarist Doctor (a) creates the rhythm and adds melodic layers to the composition while cantaor(a) (flamenco singer) provides emotional vocals, pouring raw emotions into each line. These components combine to produce an effective and moving performance that leaves an impression on the audience.

The cultural immersion that comes with seeing a flamenco performance in Barcelona goes beyond the performance itself. The option to enhance the performance with a choice of pre-and post-show activities is provided by Barcelona, which is renowned for its exciting nightlife and delectable cuisine. A memorable visit can be enhanced by exploring the quaint alleyways of the Gothic Quarter, indulging in traditional tapas, or sipping local wine.

Theater and Performing Arts

A center for theater and the performing arts in Barcelona, the vivacious capital of Catalonia in

Spain. The city, which is well-known for its diverse and vibrant theater culture that draws both locals and visitors, is also known for its rich cultural legacy and artistic flair. Every theater aficionado may find something to enjoy in Barcelona, from classic plays to modern productions. The interesting world of theater and performing arts in Barcelona will be explored in this essay, with special emphasis on its background, locations, events, and significant contributions to the arts.

Theater has a long history in Barcelona, with both Spanish and Catalan traditions having a significant influence. Street performances and religious plays were popular kinds of entertainment in the medieval era. As time went on, Barcelona saw the development of specialized performance venues as well as the growth of reputable theater organizations. Built-in 1597, the Teatre Principal is one of the city's oldest theaters and is being used today for a wide range of performances.

The city of Barcelona is home to a wide variety of theaters and performing spaces. The stunning opera and ballet performances of Barcelona's opera theatre, the Gran Teatre del Liceu, are well-known. Both artists and viewers love it because of its opulent architecture and acoustics. Another well-known location is the Teatre Nacional de Catalunya, which supports the regional theater scene by presenting a wide range of Catalan and foreign plays.

Theaters offering a variety of entertainment, such as comedic shows, musicals, and experimental plays, line the city's theater district, known as Parallel Avenue. With street performers and artists enhancing the neighborhood's artistic appeal, this busy area provides a dynamic environment. The Teatre Lliure, a well-known theater in the Montjuic neighborhood, specializes in cutting-edge and modern works that push the envelope and question accepted theatrical norms.

Throughout the year, Barcelona holds several theater events that draw visitors from all over the world. One such occasion is the Grec Festival, which takes place every year in the summer. The festival features a variety of theater, dance, music, and circus performances in several locations throughout the city. It creates a vibrant and welcoming cultural experience by providing a platform for both well-known artists and up-and-coming artists. Another notable festival is Temporada Alta, which is held in the adjacent town of Girona but draws international theater plays that frequently visit Barcelona.

A robust modern performing arts culture exists in Barcelona in addition to conventional theater. Innovative and immersive experiences are created by fusing theater, dance, music, and multimedia components throughout the city. Companies like La Fura dels Baus have won accolades from all around the world for their boundary-pushing shows that incorporate theater, acrobatics, and special effects.

The performing arts in Barcelona have benefited greatly from the playwrights and theater artists from Catalonia. Angel Guimerà, Josep Maria de Sagarra, and Sergi Belbel are just a few of the names that have shaped the Catalan theater scene's identity and story over time. Because of its rich cultural legacy and willingness to try new things, Barcelona has drawn theater companies and artists from all over the world, making it a lively and international theater destination.

Chapter 11

Practical Information

Accommodation Options

1. Luxurious Hotels: Barcelona offers a wide selection of opulent hotels with first-rate facilities and services. The Mandarin Oriental Barcelona, W Barcelona, Majestic Hotel & Spa Barcelona, and Hotel Arts Barcelona are just a few well-known names. These hotels include breathtaking vistas, exquisite dining options, spa amenities, and convenient access to popular activities.

2. Boutique Hotels: If you want a more individualized and private experience, Barcelona's boutique hotels are a great option. Hotels like the

Hotel Brummell, Hotel Neri Relais & Chateaux, and Casa Camper Hotel Barcelona provide the distinctive decor, a welcoming atmosphere, and individualized services.

3. Mid-Range Hotels: For accommodations that are comfortable without breaking the bank, mid-range hotels are a good choice for tourists on a moderate budget. Popular options in this category include Hotel 1898, Hotel Sixtytwo Barcelona, Hotel Pulitzer Barcelona, and H10 Universitat.

4. Budget Accommodations: Barcelona also has several hotels that are suitable for guests on a tight budget. Hotels like Hotel Curious, Hotel Condal, Hotel Barbara, and Hotel Lloret Ramblas offer cozy accommodations and standard amenities at affordable prices.

5. Hostels: Barcelona is renowned for its energetic hostel scene, drawing backpackers and cost-conscious tourists from all over the world.

Generator Barcelona, Sant Jordi Hostels, Kabul Party Hostel, and Yeah Barcelona Hostel are a few well-known hostels. These hostels provide lodging in dorm-style, as well as social areas and a buzzing atmosphere.

6. Apartments: Renting an apartment is a common option for families or tourists seeking a more comfortable setting. Barcelona is home to a large number of apartment rental companies and online marketplaces that provide a wide range of choices in various areas. It enables visitors to have their area, cooking amenities, and flexibility when traveling.

7. Guesthouses and Bed and Breakfasts: Barcelona boasts a large selection of lodging options that offer a warm and intimate ambiance. Popular options in this category include Casa Gracia Barcelona Hostel, Hotel Cuatro Naciones, Violeta Boutique, and Casa Balmes.

8. Vacation Rentals: Barcelona has a strong vacation rental sector where visitors can book short-term stays in individual houses, villas, or apartments. Vacation rental possibilities are abundant around the city thanks to websites like Airbnb, HomeAway, and VRBO.

9. Serviced apartments: Ideal for extended visits or business visitors, serviced apartments combine the convenience of a private apartment with the amenities of a hotel. Among the suppliers in Barcelona are Aspasios Apartments, BCN Apartment Rentals, and You Stylish City Centre Apartments.

10. Camping & Glamping: For nature lovers, Barcelona's surroundings offer several camping and glamping alternatives. Tents, caravans, and mobile homes can stay in campgrounds with amenities including Camping Barcelona, Camping 3 Estrellas, and Camping Sitges.

11. Rural lodgings: If you'd rather enjoy the countryside and stay outside of the city, Barcelona's rural lodgings provide a peaceful haven. The hotels Masia Can Canyes, Masia Can Felip, and Hotel Can Pamplona are well-liked options since they offer a tranquil setting and chances for outdoor activities.

12. House Exchanges: Travelers have the option of participating in house exchanges, where they trade residences with Barcelona inhabitants and get to know the city from the viewpoint of a local. Such exchanges are facilitated by websites like HomeExchange and Love Home Swap.

Transportation within the City

1. Metro: Barcelona's metro system makes getting around the city easy and effective. The metro connects important areas and attractions over a wide area with nine lines. On weekdays, it is open from 5 am until midnight and all night on Fridays and Saturdays.

2. Buses: The TMB (Transports Metropolitans de Barcelona), which runs a sizable bus network in Barcelona, is a major asset. It covers areas not served by the metro and has a variety of routes, including night buses. Wheelchair accessibility is provided by the bus system, which runs continuously.

3. Trams: Another dependable method of transportation in Barcelona are the tram. Tramlines connect several communities and offer a beautiful way to tour the city. From early in the morning until after midnight, the tram service is open.

4. FGC (Ferrocarrils de la Generalitat de Catalunya): FGC runs suburban trains that connect Barcelona with neighboring cities and areas. Access to well-liked tourist locations like Montserrat and Tibidabo is also made possible by the FGC lines.

5. Renfe: Is Spain's national railroad corporation and provides both local and long-distance train services. Significant rail hubs in Barcelona, including Barcelona Sants and Barcelona Estació de França, offer links to other Spanish cities and foreign locations.

6. Bicing: The public bicycle-sharing program in Barcelona. It enables locals and guests to rent bicycles for a predetermined amount of time from a variety of stations located throughout the city. Bicing promotes eco-friendly travel and provides a fit way to see Barcelona.

7. Taxis: They are widely available in Barcelona. They can be located at designated taxi stands, flagged down on the street, or reserved over the phone or through a smartphone app. The black and yellow color scheme of Barcelona's taxis makes them easy to spot.

8. Rental Cars: Barcelona is home to several automobile rental companies, making them a practical choice for tourists who want to explore the city on their own. However, keep in mind that there may be parking issues and heavy traffic in some regions.

9. Electric Scooters: In Barcelona, electric scooters are gaining popularity. Users can rent and ride electric scooters for quick trips around the city through several companies that offer scooter-sharing services.

10. Walking: Barcelona is a city that encourages pedestrians and has a lot of attractions that are close by. Walking around the city lets you take in its energetic streets, stunning architecture, and quaint neighborhoods at your speed.

11. Segway Tours: Segway tours are a novel way to see Barcelona's top attractions while taking a fun and environmentally friendly ride. You can see well-known places with a knowledgeable local guide on one of the offered guided tours.

12. Cable Cars: There are cable car systems in Barcelona, including the Montjuc Cable Car and the Port Vell Aerial Tramway, which provide scenic rides and stunning views of the city and its surroundings.

13. Ferries: The port at Barcelona offers ferry service to places close by, including the Balearic Islands and other Mediterranean ports. For individuals looking to travel the area by sea, ferries provide an alternate means of transportation.

14. Electric Tuk-tuks: As a novel mode of transportation in Barcelona, electric tuk-tuks have grown in popularity in recent years. These three-wheeled cars can maneuver through small alleyways and offer narrated tours of the city's sights.

15. trekking: For those who enjoy trekking, Barcelona's natural surroundings provide wonderful options. Numerous hiking paths with breathtaking views of Barcelona's cityscape are available in the Collserola Natural Park, which is close to the city.

16. Airport Transportation: Aerobus, local trains, taxis, and private shuttles are all excellent ways to get from Barcelona-El Prat Airport to the city center. These offerings guarantee simple access to and from the airport.

17. Motorcycle Rentals: In Barcelona, renting a motorcycle may be a fantastic experience. You can go around the city more easily and swiftly on a motorcycle by navigating the traffic.

18. Convenient Travel Cards: Barcelona offers cost-effective travel cards, such as the T-Casual card and the Hola Barcelona card, that grant unrestricted use of the city's public transportation for a predetermined period. For frequent travelers, these cards are affordable.

19. Carpooling: Apps and services for carpooling, such as BlaBlaCar and Amovens, let users share rides and save money on transportation while also encouraging a more environmentally friendly method of commuting.

20. Ride-Sharing: Barcelona is home to ride-sharing companies like Uber and Cabify, which offer a substitute for conventional taxis. Through these apps, consumers can quickly book rides and make payments on their cell phones.

Emergency Contacts

1. Emergency Services: 112 (Fire, Police, and Ambulance).In the whole European Union, dialing 112 will connect you to a general emergency line.

2. Police: 088 (Mossos d'Esquadra). The police force in Catalonia, which includes Barcelona, is called the Mossos d'Esquadra.

3. Medical Emergency: 061 for medical emergencies. In Barcelona, call 061 to reach emergency medical services. It is used to request medical assistance or an ambulance.

4. Contact information for Barcelona City Council: 010 For general inquiries or non-emergency situations, dial 010 to get in touch with the Barcelona City Council.

To make sure you have the most recent and accurate information for emergency contacts, it's always a good idea to confirm these numbers with local sources or consult the city of Barcelona's or emergency services' official websites.

Conclusion

Barcelona is a mesmerizing city that offers the ideal fusion of illustrious history, spectacular architecture, dynamic culture, and breathtaking natural beauty. Barcelona has something to offer everyone, regardless of your interests in art, history, food, or relaxing on the beach.

The spectacular Sagrada Familia, Park Güell, and Casa Batlló, among other well-known structures in the city, are must-see sights that exhibit the talent of renowned architect Antoni Gaud. You can fully experience the distinctive charm and lively ambiance of the city by exploring the winding lanes of the Gothic Quarter and strolling down the well-known pedestrian thoroughfare of La Rambla.

The Picasso Museum and the Joan Miró Foundation are only two examples of Barcelona's booming art culture. Countless eateries, tapas bars, and food markets serving delectable Catalan and foreign cuisine make up the city's exceptional gastronomic offerings.

The stunning beaches of Barceloneta are the ideal place for nature lovers to unwind and enjoy the warm Mediterranean sun. You can take a day excursion to the breathtaking vistas of Montserrat or escape to the charming Montjuic mountains, both of which are close by.

Additionally, throughout the year, a variety of cultural events and celebrations bring Barcelona's festive spirit to life. The lively celebrations, including the eye-catching La Mercè Festival and the exciting Festa Major de Gràcia, highlight the city's vivacious character and sense of community.

Barcelona can be congested, especially during the busiest travel seasons, so keep that in mind. Plan your itinerary, purchase tickets for popular attractions in advance, and be ready for potential lines to ensure that you get the most out of your trip.

Printed in Great Britain
by Amazon

30821331R00126